Advanced Introduction to American Foreign Policy

Advanced Introduction to

American Foreign Policy

LOCH K. JOHNSON

School of Public and International Affairs, University of Georgia, USA

Elgar Advanced Introductions

Cheltenham, UK • Northampton, MA, USA

Published by
Edward Elgar Publishing Limited
The Lypiatts
15 Lansdown Road
Cheltenham
Glos GL50 2JA
UK

Edward Elgar Publishing, Inc.
William Pratt House
9 Dewey Court
Northampton
Massachusetts 01060
USA

A catalogue record for this book
is available from the British Library

Library of Congress Control Number: 2021939232

Printed on elemental chlorine free (ECF)
recycled paper containing 30% Post-Consumer Waste

ISBN 978 1 80088 172 3 (cased)
ISBN 978 1 80088 174 7 (paperback)
ISBN 978 1 80088 173 0 (eBook)

Printed and bound in the USA

For
Les Aspin
Member of Congress, Secretary of Defense, mentor, friend

Contents

PART V   THE CHALLENGES AHEAD

Preface

The purpose of this book is to enhance an understanding of how the United States interacts with the rest of the world. The study of this topic must take into account America's constitutional framework, which is the nation's fundamental blueprint for the making of foreign and domestic policy. Important, too, is the story of how U.S. global activities have unfolded over the decades, from the earliest days of the Republic beginning in 1787 – an era of sailing ships and muskets – to the contemporary world of rapid transportation, instant communications, the swift spread of pandemics, environmental degradation, and the proliferation of powerful weapons.

Further, this book examines how officials in Washington, D.C. go about selecting specific instruments to carry out America's foreign policy objectives, such as diplomacy, trade agreements, secretive covert actions, or the use of military force. These three aspects of American foreign policy – constitutional underpinnings, historical evolution, and the instruments of policy – lie at the heart of the chapters that follow.

The book also uses a levels-of-analysis perspective on foreign policy that highlights the significance of three levels where decisions are shaped: the international setting, the world stage where nations jostle for security and advantage; domestic politics, where a complex array of interest groups attempts to influence foreign policy in Washington; and the individual level, where influences arise from personal styles of policy officials in high office, interest group lobbying, and citizens at the ballot box.

In Part I of the book, the chapters begin with a broad introduction to the subject of American foreign policy. This section addresses the international objectives and approaches pursued by officials in Washington;

offers an analytic construct for the study of foreign policy; and ends with a look at how the nation's Constitution continues to shape America's relations overseas even now – more than 234 years after that document was drafted. Part II provides a historical backdrop vital for understanding the evolution of contemporary foreign policy. Part III explores the institutions and individuals responsible for shaping America's international pursuits. In Part IV, the narrative turns to the question of how policy-makers use each key instrument of foreign policy, such as war-making, diplomacy, and clandestine operations. Lastly, Part V explores some fresh approaches to addressing global challenges.

Finally, the author would like to thank the talented team at Edward Elgar Publishing for their guidance in the preparation of this book, including editor Stephen Harris, who encouraged the project from the beginning; Marina Bowgen and Betty Ruck for their sure guidance along the way; and Geraldine Lyons for her outstanding copy-editing.

PART I

Introduction

1 The United States as a world power

The terrorist attacks against the United States on September 11, 2001 (a tragic day for the nation, remembered as "9/11") underscored, vividly and painfully, the importance of global threats to the nation. International terrorists killed almost 3,000 Americans within minutes by flying hijacked commercial airlines into skyscrapers in New York City and at the Pentagon, across the Potomac River from Washington, D.C. It was now all too clear that dangers, once seemingly far away, across the protective moats of the Atlantic and Pacific Oceans, could suddenly arrive on America's doorstep. The next time terrorists attacked the United States, they might well have at their disposal nuclear, biological, chemical, or radiological weapons, instantly inflicting casualties in the hundreds of thousands, perhaps even millions.

America's economic relations with the rest of the world have also undergone a significant evolution since the end of the Second World War. In the 1980s, expanding market opportunities across the latitudes led to a much larger volume of worldwide commercial activity. Barriers that once impeded the global flow of capital, goods, services, information, and technology have given way to new trading relationships. In recent years, for instance, the American automobile company General Motors has built 70 percent of its vehicles outside the United States, with 11 joint ventures in China alone.

Yet with increased trading has come growing competition for the United States in the international marketplace. America remains an economic behemoth and accounts for a quarter of the world's gross domestic product; however, it has lost much of its economic strength relative to its status even a decade ago, when the U.S. economy accounted for one-third of the world's GDP. As the forces of globalization continue to expand, no nation stands alone in the world; all are woven together by commerce, communications, and travel. Each nation has had to adapt to this new, interdependent, and complex setting.

Objectives

Foreign policy may be defined as a nation's pursuit of objectives in the world through relationships with other countries, international organizations, and various factions – including well-organized ethnic groups, like the Bosnians in the Balkans; or powerful interest groups, like the farmers of France. Governments hope to translate national aspirations into realities through the use of various instruments of power, whether diplomats, spies, or troops – and sometimes all three at once. Foreign policy is influenced by a nation's system of values: its political and economic norms, as well as cultural and moral beliefs. These values shape "grand strategy," that is, a nation's global objectives (ends) and its choice of tools (means) to pursue these goals.

Nations actively try to shape their destiny. The primary foreign policy objectives of the United States include the physical protection of its citizens and territory, as well as the economic prosperity of its people. Improvements in the quality of life, including a pollution-free environment and cures for disease, are important, too; and another goal for some nations is the advancement of human rights across the globe. Public opinion polls conducted over the past 50 years have consistently indicated, though, that America's pursuit of security and prosperity garners widespread support among citizens, while the goals of quality of life and human rights have attracted less unanimity of support.

Peace and security

During the Administration of President Ronald Reagan (1981–1989), the State Department emphasized the importance of "seeking to protect the security of our nation and its institutions, as well as those our allies and friends." President Barack Obama (2009–2017) similarly emphasized in a speech that his foremost responsibility was "to forge an America that is safer, a world that is more secure … ." Citizens of the United States often have vastly different views about foreign policy. On one matter, however, most everyone agrees: the government must ensure the safety of the American people.

So far, humanity's record for establishing peace and security has been checkered. Most of the time, a majority of states have been at peace with one another – a remarkable, but seldom remarked upon fact. Yet, throughout the roughly 5,500 years of recorded history, the world has enjoyed only about 300 years (off and on) in which no nation has been at war anywhere on the planet. During the Second World War, over 60 million people perished; and nearly 30 million have died in armed conflicts since then.

Some historians have labeled the Cold War (1945–1991) as "the long peace," because the two nuclear-armed superpowers – the United States and the Soviet Union – avoided a Third World War that might have destroyed the world. Yet, this period was anything but peaceful for many people. As the Cold War wound down during the years from 1989 to 1991, one out of every four countries was at war. In 1989, the year in which the Berlin Wall was torn down, about 500,000 people lost their lives in violent conflicts in Central America, Sudan, Eritrea, the Middle East, Northern Ireland, Southern Africa, and Sri Lanka. And whether in the form of terrorist attacks or more traditional battlefield confrontations, war – like disease – remains a major nemesis of the human race. No wonder peace and security rank as the primary goals of American foreign policy, as for other nations, however elusive this hope has been.

Economic prosperity

The economic well-being of the American people is another core objective of U.S. foreign policy. In 1993, the Clinton Administration (1993–2001) stressed that "practitioners of statecraft [must not] forget that their ultimate goal is to improve the daily lives of the American people." President Clinton stressed the nurturing of a robust economy at home and abroad to achieve a higher standard of living, although his orientation toward economic prosperity soon began to take second place as crises related to peace and security began to mount in Africa and the Balkans.

American foreign policy is inextricably bound to global economic conditions. As the Carnegie Endowment for International Peace has pointed out, foreign policy can raise or lower the cost of a home mortgage, create a new job, or eliminate one you presently have. The high unemployment rate that ravaged the economy of the United States from 2008 to 2012 (a period known as the Great Recession) was, in part, a function of the world's slumping economy. A setback in Washington's political relations with Moscow can harm the American farmer dearly through the loss of grain sales to Russia. Money flows across international boundaries like water, with U.S. banks insuring European and other foreign banks – and suffering the consequences if they fail.

Quality of life

A third objective of America's foreign policy has been to find solutions to a cluster of lifestyle challenges that threaten the future of the United States and every other country. Of high priority are protecting the world environment from the dangers of global warming, as well as the pollution of this planet's land, air, and seas. Vital, too, are better safeguards against the spread of pandemics, as with the COVID-19 virus that swept the world in 2020.

Human rights

A fourth objective seeks the elimination of human rights violations around the world. The Carter Administration (1977–1981) stressed that every individual, within the United States and abroad, has inherent rights and a special dignity. For many people, freedom from government repression in every corner of the planet registers high on their hierarchy of personal wishes.

These primary goals of American foreign policy – physical safety, economic prosperity, quality of life, and human rights – are difficult to achieve. Debates over which of these goals should be energetically embraced by the United States reveal deep-seated disagreements among citizens. The matter of physical safety is often just taken for granted by citizens – a given when it comes to government responsibilities. What they are more likely to address when queried by pollsters is the more practical question of bread on the table – economic well-being. The responses of Americans in recent polls indicate that their chief concern was the creation of jobs within the United States. Foreign policy objectives beyond economic prosperity usually garnered significantly less support. Here are some illustrations of what percentage of those polled in 2018 believed a particular foreign policy goal was important:

- Lowering unemployment: 77%
- Preventing the spread of terrorism: 54%
- Preventing Iran from acquiring a nuclear weapon: 52%
- Combating the impacts of climate change: 37%
- Promoting human rights in the Middle East and North Africa: 31%

Instruments

The United States, as with every other country, is forced to accept a gap between policy aspirations and what can actually be accomplished in a world of competing nations and factions. No nation has a monopoly on oil, technological innovation, or control of the seas. None has impermeable borders resistant to pollution, global warming, pandemics, illicit drugs, or illegal immigrants. None has a foolproof system of defense against foreign military or terrorist attacks.

Each nation gauges its capabilities and crafts approaches to foreign affairs that are designed to help advance its interests in the world, while avoiding military defeat and bankruptcy. These approaches are referred to in this book as foreign policy instruments, an umbrella term that includes: intelligence gathering; diplomacy; war-making; secret interventions abroad (covert action); economic statecraft, and the "soft power" influences of ethics and culture. Together, they make up a nation's power, that is, its ability to convince other nations and factions to accept its international objectives – or, at least, not to oppose them.

Intelligence

The gathering and assessment of information about global events and conditions is often referred to as intelligence collection-and-analysis. This instrument is presented here first, because all of the other instruments depend for their success on having reliable information about the world.

Diplomacy

This instrument involves the art of adjusting disputes between nations and factions through formal and informal negotiations.

War-making

Sometimes presidents turn to the threat, or use, of open military intervention – the war power – as a means for hastening the resolution of an international problem. Since 1787, the United States has been free of military engagements abroad only in 19 years.

Secret operations

Another approach used by the United States to advance its foreign policy agenda is the use of covert actions by the Central Intelligence Agency (CIA). These shadowy activities include the use of secret propaganda, along with political, economic, and paramilitary (war-like) activities.

Economic statecraft

Trade and aid, forms of diplomatic activity that focus on the commercial and financial side of foreign policy, have also served as key instruments in America's pursuit of its global objectives. They are often referred to as economic statecraft.

Moral and cultural suasion

Supreme Court Justice William O. Douglas once observed that the United States was admired abroad not "so much for our B-52 bombers and for our atomic stockpile, but ... for the First Amendment and the freedom of people to speak and believe and to write, have fair trials." Here, in his view, was the "great magnet" that made America a respected world leader: the power of moral suasion, winning friends abroad by virtue of setting a good example as a vibrant democracy. Moreover, cultural suasion – winning friends abroad because of a nation's attractive social attributes (Hollywood movies, for example) – can be an additional magnet drawing the people of other nations toward the United States. Youth the world over wear jeans made in Los Angeles, and they drink Coca-Cola from Atlanta and play video games developed in Silicon Valley.

Philosophies

Idealism

Many government officials in the United States have been drawn to the power of moral principle in international affairs, which is part of a tradition of liberalism or idealism in international affairs. In international relations theory, liberals advocate the resolution of international conflicts by way of international law, negotiations through international organizations, and the promotion of collective security arrangements. Liberals also place an emphasis on human rights; and they express a sense of optimism about the chances for peaceful interdependence among states.

Neoliberalism

A related approach is neoliberalism. Like liberalism, this philosophy also advocates the worldwide development of democracy, open markets, and free trade; but it adds the idea that these objectives can be best achieved through the adoption of international regimes. Regimes are written agreements entered into by states that seek mutual cooperation for the benefit of all signatories. The General Agreement on Tariffs and Trade (GATT), for example, established important international economic relationships among states that began in the 1940s and lasted 50 years, until replaced by the World Trade Organization (WTO) in 1995. The neoliberal approach embedded in the GATT initiative was to adopt the use of negotiated contractual understandings – not just formal international organizations with detailed rules and procedures, as a liberal theorist would advocate – to advance economic prosperity between nations.

Social constructivism

Another school of thought is social constructivism, a point of view related to liberalism and neoliberalism in its expression of optimism about the chances for improvements in global integration and peace. This school concentrates on the questions of how social norms, ideas, and images can influence international relations; and the importance of how nations think of themselves and their values in comparison with other nations. Liberals and idealists, neoliberals, and social constructivists are optimists who advocate the goals of the international community and a sense of fair play in global affairs, along with the promotion of worldwide egalitarianism and economic prosperity.

Realism

In contrast, some students of international affairs who are known as "realists" remain skeptical about the value of law in international relations, or the utility of international organizations and ethical considerations. They believe that a state's external relations should rest more prudently on a foundation of military and economic strength. If the liberals or idealists are optimistic about world affairs, the realists are pessimistic. They are said to practice *realpolitik*, an approach to international relations that emphasizes practical over ethical or ideological considerations.

The foreign policy views of official in the United States are commonly a mixture of idealism and realism. Professor Joseph S. Nye Jr. refers to an ability to combine these instincts into an effective strategy as "smart power."

Notes

On the conduct of American foreign policy, see John Lewis Gaddis, *George F. Kennan: An American Life* (New York: Penguin, 2012); Hans J. Morgenhau, *Politics Among Nations: The Struggle for Power and Peace* (New York: Knopf, 1973, originally published in 1948); and Joseph S. Nye, Jr., *The Paradox of American Power* (New York: Oxford University Press, 2002), as well as his *Soft Power: The Means to Success in World Politics* (New York: Public Affairs, 2004). George Kennan was America's most famous diplomat in the era since the end of the Second World War. For additional overviews on U.S. policies abroad and how they are shaped at home, see Dean Rusk (a former U.S. Secretary of State), with Richard Rusk and Daniel S. Papp, *As I Saw It* (New York: Norton, 1990); and G. John Ikenberry, Thomas J. Knock, Anne-Marie Slaughter, and Tony Smith, *The Crisis of American Foreign Policy: Wilsonianism in the Twenty-First Century* (Princeton, NJ: Princeton University Press, 2008). On the levels of analysis approach to the study of foreign policy, see Kenneth N. Waltz, *Man, the State, and War* (New York: Cambridge University Press, 1959). Various philosophies of foreign policy are reviewed in Steven W. Hook and Christopher M. Jones, eds., *Routledge Handbook of American Foreign Policy* (New York: Routledge, 2012). For polling on the views of U.S. citizens regarding their foreign policy preferences, the Chicago Council of Foreign Relations, as well as the Carnegie Endowment for International Peace, regularly publish public opinion findings.

An analytic framework

The influences on foreign policy decisions that arise in America's pursuit of its global objectives are summarized in Figure 2.1. The purpose of this analytic "roadmap" is to provide an outline of the complexities that confront the United States in its relations with the rest of the world. Figure 2.1 emphasizes the importance of historical and constitutional antecedents; the tension between the executive and legislative institutions of governance; and the sundry human conditions that stand between the decision-maker and the selection of foreign policy instruments.

Historians and social scientists have long debated the question of which is more important in the momentous decisions that shape the course of world affairs: the presence of a "great leader" – say, a Washington, Napoleon, or Lenin – or the special circumstances of the time that forced action, such as the British tyranny perpetrated against the American colonists in the 1700s. The arrows in Figure 2.1 point to the proper conclusion: decisions, large and small, are the result of a complex inter-play between the psychological orientations and personal attributes of individual decision-makers, on the one hand, *and* the historical and insti-tutional situation they face at the time, on the other hand. The pressure of events, and human perceptions about these events, lead to a reaction: a decision. As depicted in the figure, international and national historical experiences (among them, the provisions of the Constitution) influence the personal development and worldview of individual decision-makers. In turn, as these decision-makers pursue a grand strategy, they operate in a bargaining environment and interact with multiple governmental insti-tutions and societal groups as they select instruments or tools of foreign policy they wish to use in the pursuit of the nation's foreign policy goals.

Figure 2.1 simplifies an intricate reality. Analysts have stressed the com-plexity by contrasting foreign policy decisions with a game of chess. In chess, there are only six distinct pieces, a handful of rules, and a board

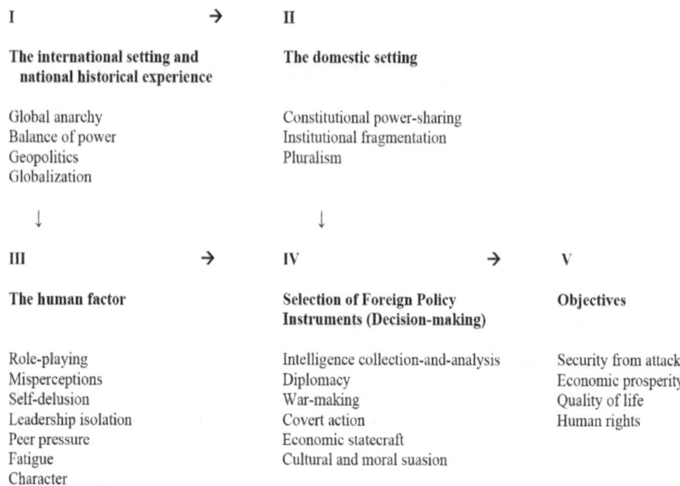

Figure 2.1   An analytic framework for the study of American foreign policy

that is just eight-by-eight units square. Yet even in this game, the number of possible sequences of moves is incredibly large: some 10 to the 120th power – essentially, infinity. Chess is simple, though, compared to the sequence of possible moves available to policymakers in real-life situations, say, the movement of naval ships and ground soldiers against an enemy in time of war. Compared to a chess board, oceans and battle-grounds are vast. Figure 2.1 underscores the complexity of foreign policy. Central to the construct are the three levels of foreign policy analysis: the international setting, the national setting, and the individual.

International setting

On one point most scholars of foreign policy stand in agreement: the world is essentially anarchical, in the sense that no world government with centralized authority exists. This fragmented international setting makes cooperation among nations a challenge. Although factions (terrorist groups, for instance), international and regional organizations like the UN and NATO, and multinational corporations (MNCs) have become increasingly important entities in the world, the nation remains the basic organizational unit in international affairs, as fundamental to an understanding of foreign policy as the atom is to physics. A nation may be defined as a gathering together of individuals under a common leadership, or government, in control of a well-defined territorial space. Normally, the citizens of a nation share a cultural identity as well, including a common language and an allegiance to a distinctive flag and national anthem. A nation thus has both territorial and psychological dimensions.

Balance of power

Central to the realist's view of foreign policy is the idea of balance of power. According to this theory, if one nation becomes too dominant militarily, it will attempt to manipulate – or even conquer – other nations. Therefore, vulnerable nations will form coalitions among themselves, designed to prevent the threatening outsider from achieving military superiority over the rest. A balance of power approach to foreign policy shaped America's response to the global challenge of Marxist-Leninist ideology advocated during the Cold War by communists in the Soviet Union and China, along with their allies. This communist ideology was in obvious conflict with America's fundamental beliefs in democracy, individual rights, and free enterprise.

As a check against the spread of communism, U.S. policymakers adopted the posture of containment. This policy rested on a conviction that the leaders of the Soviet Union were determined to disrupt the international equilibrium; that they wished to dominate the globe, just as Hitler had aspired. Sometimes the Soviet approach was to use force in expanding the communist empire, as in Eastern Europe and Manchuria, but more often Moscow adopted subtler techniques involving secret propaganda operations and other "active measures" (the Russian term for secret intelligence operations) in support of Marxist "wars of liberation" in the developing world, as in Vietnam and Angola.

To counter this threat, the Truman Administration (1945–1953) embraced a steadfast resistance against Soviet aggression in Greece, Turkey, and other places around the globe. Important, too, was the building of alliances in the West for collective security, most notably the North Atlantic Treaty Organization (NATO), established in 1949 and comprised of the

United States, Canada, and key European nations. The Cold War was sustained by the core belief in Washington and other Western capitals that the Soviets had to be fenced in by a coalition of democratic nations prepared to use political, economic, covert action, and even (if necessary) overt military means to halt the communist advance.

With the end of the Cold War in 1991, the world changed dramatically from a bipolar stand-off between the two superpowers – Russia and the United States – to a unipolar world in which the United States had become the most dominant nation in the world. Efforts to counter U.S. influence, as predicted by the balance of power theory, failed to material-ize in any concerted manner. Only the nations of Europe had the capacity to coalesce against America, but, correctly, they looked upon the United States as a friend, not a threat, and saw no need to rally against the world's leading power with a new military defense pact of their own.

Geopolitics

Students of foreign policy rarely dispute the belief that geography can play a significant role in the relationships among nations. For instance, under-standing the importance of a strong U.S. presence in the Atlantic and Pacific Oceans to protect trading lanes, Admiral Alfred Thayer Mahan wrote persuasively about the need for a "blue-water" (ocean-going) U.S. Navy in the late 1800s. Geopolitics, that aspect of foreign policy influ-enced by the number, size, strength, location, and topography of nations, is a prominent feature in the planning of foreign policy officials.

Large nations with imposing arsenals have often insisted on a "sphere of influence" reaching out from their borders, into which other nations might tread only at the peril of triggering a military reaction. Since the proclamation of the Monroe Doctrine in 1823, the United States has claimed the Western Hemisphere as its sphere of influence. During the Cold War, Western geo-strategists warned that the communist nations would attempt to expand their spheres of influence, moving steadily from one contiguous territory to another around the world. This dread was referred to in Washington as the "domino theory." First, one domino – say, Albania – would fall under the weight of a communist onslaught, then the next and the next, toppling one after another as in the child's game until, at last, the chain reaction reached the last domino: the United States itself.

The chief weakness of the domino theory lies in its assumption that somehow the toppling of one domino will somehow lead inevitably to the toppling of adjacent dominos. History would suggest, on the contrary, that there is nothing preordained about anything, and that nations can be resistant to outside threats. The next "domino" may well have a strong economy, a potent military defense, or simply a robust belief in nationalism that finds utterly repugnant any form of colonialism, Marxism, or other "ism" that attempts to topple them. In recent decades, sweeping changes in modern transportation and communications, as well as more rapid means for delivering military strikes across national borders, have diminished the significance of geopolitical influences. Nevertheless, considerations of geography and natural resources sometimes enter the picture when the United States weighs its foreign policy interests and options, as shown below.

Globalization

The growth of multinational corporations and international organizations; a rising sense of common identity among groups in different nations, such as Russian and American scientists issuing a joint statement against nuclear weapons, or the youth of the world joined in devotion to the same rock bands, movie stars, hair styles, retro-clothing, or, on the policy side, serious environmental reforms; interwoven commercial transactions across borders and a shared concern about the rippling effects of recession and inflation; cultural and academic exchanges; common international transportation carriers and channels of communication; common concern about the transmission of global diseases – indeed, the entire intricate interplay among modern nations has made transnational forces ever more important on a world stage characterized by a complex international interdependence or globalization. Nothing demonstrated this connectivity so vividly and gruesomely as the COVID-19 pandemic, as it skipped rapidly across the continents, moving outward from Wuhan, China, in 2020.

International television broadcasts, the Internet, tweeting, blogs, and other forms of "new media" are a central part of the trend toward international integration. Television, for example, brought the Vietnam War into the homes of millions of Americans, who from the comfort of their dens viewed the battlefield slaughter with a growing revulsion. Today, when terrorists strike in New York City, Washington, D.C., or Detroit; when

U.S. Marines are killed in Iraq or Afghanistan; when earthquakes level Haiti; when asphyxiated pelicans wash ashore in Louisiana, drenched in oil from a broken rig in the Gulf, television and Internet news outlets inform the public immediately, often with disturbing photographs and video footage. The quickness by which televised images of international events enter the White House Situation Room and other high government offices, and well as the living rooms of citizens across the country, is sometimes referred to as the CNN effect, stemming from the 24/7 coverage of world affairs by the Cable News Network.

Some observers see in this knitting together of a global communion of citizens an opportunity for a new world order that could replace the anarchy and warfare common to the current, still-fragmented system of nations. This "one-worlder" school of thought hopes to create fresh transnational friendship ties and commonalities that will eventually bring lasting peace to "spaceship earth." Others remain skeptical and emphasize what they see as a more likely outcome: the endurance of global competition and strife among nations and factions.

Domestic setting

"Foreign policy is domestic policy, and domestic policy is foreign policy," observed Jake Sullivan, the new National Security Adviser for the Biden Administration, which entered office in 2021. He was pointing to the rich interplay between foreign policy and domestic politics. Of special interest among the influences within the United States that affect foreign policy are the nation's historical experiences, especially the constitutional underpinnings of U.S. government, along with the contemporary institutional arrangement for governance and America's pluralist politics.

Constitutional power-sharing

The U.S. Constitution, the blueprint for government drafted by the American founders in 1787, has had a profound influence on the conduct of foreign policy. The venerable phrase usually invoked to describe this framework is the "separation of powers." Political scientist Richard E. Neustadt offered a more accurate description, though, when he stressed the reality of separate institutions *sharing* power in the United States. The authority to make war or to approve treaties, for example, requires participation by both the legislative and executive branches, with periodic arbitration by the judicial branch of government. Article I of the Constitution gives Congress – America's parliament – the power to declare war, yet Article II names the president as the commander-in-chief. When such powers are shared, tensions and ambiguities arise within the government. Who ultimately will assume the responsibility to commit the nation to war, or a binding trade agreement with another country? By spreading the authority for such decisions across governmental institutions, the Constitution pitted one branch against another. This is precisely what the founders had in mind as a check against any one branch – especially the presidency – from becoming too strong and threatening to the principles of democratic government.

Institutional fragmentation

Some observers fear that these institutional arrangements for foreign policy have led to excessive fragmentation within the government: the dispersal of power too broadly. For example, critics opposed to the involvement of Congress in foreign affairs complain about its 535 elected representatives, each a would-be secretary of state on Capitol Hill, as well as the proliferation of investigative subcommittees and congressional hearings, which together sum to a heavy surcharge on the time of the actual secretaries of state and defense. In contrast, others wring their hands over what they see as power lodged too exclusively with the executive branch – the chief concern that animated the authors of the Constitution. Critics of strong centralized power in the presidency complain, as well, about slippery grants of authority passed from the White House to the Central Intelligence Agency (CIA), the Department of Defense (DoD), and other agencies and departments in an elusive shell game within the executive branch that cloud the ability of lawmakers to track the course of American foreign policy.

Political pluralism

As if the institutional fragmentation of government agencies were an insufficient complication, the United States also has an open, pluralist society that further diffuses the number of groups and individuals able to influence foreign policy decisions. The term "pluralism" is meant to characterize the existence of multiple centers of power within the United States. These power centers are found not only within the government but across the wide land – a bewildering assortment of organizations of various stripes, some with strong foreign policy beliefs that they press upon decision-makers, sometimes with marked success. Among the most prominent are the Democratic and Republican parties, which frequently – and often shrilly – disagree with one another's international objectives. Critics argue that the influence of these power centers (Wall Street, for another, or the Council on Foreign Relations in New York City) has become too great, amplified by the campaign funds they provide to office-holders in exchange for foreign policy favors.

Individual setting

In his memoir, diplomat George F. Kennan lamented that foreign policy scholarship had been distorted by an "under-estimation of psychological and political reactions – of such things as fear, ambition, insecurity, jealousy, and perhaps even boredom – as prime movers of events." The emotions, personal idiosyncrasies, distorted or false information, and other psychological vulnerabilities of individuals in high office also play a part in determining America's activities abroad.

Role-playing

The type of office occupied by a decision-maker may cause him or her to hold and implement views traditional to that office. Critical of the negative effects of this "role-playing," an experienced government offi-cial once bemoaned the "curator mentality" at the Department of State. According to this critique, regardless of their personal views, when State Department officials inherit the job of a country desk officer, they are expected to keep existing U.S. policy toward the foreign nation intact, just as they find it, "carefully protected under glass, untampered with, and dusted," as if the diplomats were but museum curators. Role-playing is hardly an infallible predictor, though, of how officials will behave. During the Obama Administration, for instance, Secretary of Defense Robert M. Gates extolled the virtues of having a stronger Department of State and placed more of an emphasis on diplomacy rather than military power – not always the Pentagon's view.

Misperceptions

How one perceives reality can be more important than reality itself. Foreign policy officials have often erred because of distorted perceptions: a failure to accurately comprehend events and conditions in the world around them. This happened to officials during the second Bush Administration, with their misperceptions about the presence of weapons of mass destruction (WMD) in Iraq. The Administration went to war against Iraq based on the false hypothesis that it had WMD and intended to use them against the United States. A variety of psychological orientations contribute to this common pathology, including the following human flaws.

Self-delusion

One important source of misperception is self-delusion, as officials brush aside – or bend – facts that fail to conform to their preconceived worldview. A former chief CIA analyst, Dr. Ray S. Cline, remembers that in 1966 American policymakers started to "lose interest in an objective description of the outside world and were beginning to scramble for evidence that they were going to win the war in Vietnam." By 1969, Cline recalls, the pathology had reached disease proportions, lasting through 1973, when "there was almost total dissent from the real world around us." Presidents Lyndon B. Johnson and Richard M. Nixon found it hard to face the fact that the United States was losing the war in Indochina.

Leadership isolation

An example of leadership isolation occurred during the second Bush Administration as the president contemplated war against Iraq. Three important agencies in the U.S. intelligence community (the Bureau of Intelligence and Research in the State Department, the U.S. Air Force, and the Energy Department) prepared reports that questioned the likelihood of WMD in that nation, yet the president never closely examined these reports or invited representatives of these agencies to the Oval Office (the "Oval") before making his decision to launch a U.S. invasion in 2003.

Peer pressure

Reality can be distorted, too, by a phenomenon of interaction displayed by small groups, labeled "groupthink" by psychologist Irving L. Janis. This term refers to a tendency for individuals in some groups to cast aside a realistic appraisal of alternative courses of action in favor of high cohesiveness among the group's membership. It becomes more important for them to conform to group expectations – peer-group pressure – than to be correct. On the basis of his study of the CIA's covert attack against Cuba in 1961, Janis concluded: "The failure of Kennedy's inner circle to detect any of the false assumptions behind the Bay of Pigs invasion plan can be at least partially accounted for by the group's tendency to seek concurrence at the expense of seeking information, critical appraisal, and debate." As a result, this covert action failed completely.

Fatigue

The higher up the organizational ladder, the more harried an official is apt to be. A study of American policymakers during the war in Vietnam pointed to executive fatigue as a significant influence on decision-making. Exhaustion stemming from too many responsibilities has a deadening effect on clear thinking.

Character

A policymaker's basic personality traits or character, as evolved from childhood, can also have a profound if often subtle influence on foreign policy decisions. Some research indicates, for instance, that a willingness of some individuals in high office to use military force as a policy option is tied to their "high-dominance" personalities. Individuals with this type of personality insist on "running the show," imposing their will forcefully on subordinates, berating them, and often ignoring them altogether as they set policy directions by themselves.

The student of foreign affairs who ignores or rejects the influences of the individual decision-maker in foreign policy risks the danger of overlooking strong undercurrents in the shaping of America's relations abroad. Foreign policy is more than global interactions and domestic politics; it can involve internal battles of the psyche as well.

The perspective of the individual on American foreign policy is shaped significantly not only by personal experience, but by the nation's historical experiences, the focus of the next chapter.

Notes

For additional reading on the concept of grand strategy, see Williamson Murray and Mark Grimsley, "Introduction: On Strategy," in Williamson Murray, MacGregor Knox, and Alvin Bernstein, eds., *The Making of Strategy: Rulers, States, and War* (New. York: Cambridge University, 1994): 1–23. For a classic statement on balance of power, see Arnold Wolfers, "The Balance of Power in Theory and Practice," *Naval War College Review* 11 (January 1959): 1–19. See, also, Irving L. Janis, *Groupthink*, 2nd ed. (Boston, MA: Houghton Mifflin, 1982); and Richard E. Neustadt, *Presidential Power* (New York: Wiley, 1960). On the curator mentality: James C. Thomson, "Vietnam: An Autopsy," *Atlantic Monthly* (April 1968): 47; and the Cline quote is from Roy Godson, ed., *Intelligence Requirements for the 1980s: Analysis and Estimates* (Washington, D.C.: National Strategy Information Center, 1980): 79. Louis Fisher provides important insights into the relationship between the executive and legislative branches of government in his *President and Congress: Power and Policy* (New York: Free Press, 1972).

PART II

The influences of history

3 The formative years of American foreign policy

Operating under a novel and untested constitutional framework, militarily weak, and wary of much more powerful countries on the European continent, the United States moved cautiously in the conduct of its early foreign policy. Yet conflict with the powers of Europe sometimes proved hard for the United States to avoid: run-ins with France in an on-again, off-again relationship; with the British, who also alternated between amity and enmity toward the erstwhile colonies and, in 1812, humiliated the Americans with a devastating military attack against the nation's capital; and with Spanish soldiers along America's eastern seaboard.

Now and then the United States broke its rule of detachment from foreign engagements and sought out policy advantages abroad. For example, President Thomas Jefferson viewed the buying of the Louisiana territory from France in 1803 as an opportunity to expand the United States, and, in 1846, war with Mexico held out the prospect of gaining additional land on the American frontier. For the most part, however, the founders and those who followed in their footsteps pursued a policy of isolation from political and military entanglements overseas. Yet, at the same time, the young nation's leaders were always on the lookout for beneficial economic opportunities abroad and, in addition, they were pleased to accept military assistance from France for protection against England and vice versa. With the advent of the Spanish-American War in 1898, these efforts to remain isolated changed dramatically; the United States began to look outward to the wider world. Before the nation assumed this more global perspective, however, it faced many challenges from stronger nations.

Nation-building, 1776–1897

The contemporary relations of the United States overseas have important antecedents in the nation's early history. Over the years, Americans have displayed an uneasy vacillation between indifference and attraction toward the rest of the world, depending on the perceptions held at any given time by leaders and the public about the possible risks and rewards associated with foreign involvement. Absent a strong army and navy, groping for an identity, facing an uncertain future, Americans during the nation's early years were chiefly concerned about shielding the fragile tendrils of their new democracy. In the interests of self-preservation, the new nation struck a posture of aloofness from the wars and wrangling of the European continent, a policy stance that later generations would refer to as isolationism.

In this aspiration for separation from the maelstrom of European and other international perils, the United States was blessed by good fortune. The foremost advantage was geographic: the protection afforded by the wide moats of the Atlantic and Pacific Oceans. America would gingerly seek out commercial opportunities with the contentious powers of Europe, but would avoid political and military "entanglements" – a favorite expression of America's founders. This splendid isolation, however, was proving to be neither splendid nor isolated. The United States increasingly understood that it needed commercial markets abroad if it were going to prosper as a nation. Attempts to establish trading partnerships, though, led to political and even military entanglements, however much America's leaders tried to keep trade separate from world politics and military affairs. The evolving rule of thumb for dealing with other nations was isolationism, yes, but not when a timely military alliance might benefit the United States, as with the French during the War of Independence; isolationism, yes, except when commercial opportunities abroad might help entrepreneurs in Boston, New York, and Savannah sell their furs, fish, grain, tobacco, and textiles overseas and thereby buoy the nation's economy.

The War of 1812 proved to be a stunning setback for the infant nation. Within two years, though, both London and Washington had grown weary of the war-induced tax burdens and the rising battlefield casualties arising from this conflict. They signed the Treaty of Ghent, bringing this second war between America and Britain to an end in 1814. America focused again on its main foreign policy interests: securing the territorial integrity of the world's first constitutional democracy and nurturing its commercial activities. These objectives were highlighted by President James Monroe's State of the Union Address of 1823. The speech was a case of the pupil sternly wagging his finger at the headmaster. In this most heralded of all American foreign policy pronouncements, subsequently labeled the Monroe Doctrine, the president warned the capitals of the Old World that the nations of the Western Hemisphere were "henceforth not to be considered as subjects for future colonization by any European power." The hubris displayed in these words was quite remarkable for a weak, fledgling nation.

Next on America's agenda was the prospect of gaining more land in the southwest and along the Pacific coast. Westward expansion was viewed as the nation's "manifest [that is, self-evident] destiny," a bequest supposedly granted by God. The United States declared war against Mexico in 1846, acquiring in the peace treaty of Guadalupe Hidalgo in 1948 all of New Mexico, California, and an extension of the Texas boundary to the Rio Grande. Once at the gateway to the Pacific, Asia soon beckoned to the restless spirit of southern cotton growers, western fur trappers, business entrepreneurs, adventurers, and missionaries.

By the mid-nineteenth century, the United States had established two quite different postures toward the world: keeping Europe at a distance, while reaching out to Asia for trade and missionary work. Isolation, on the one hand; involvement, on the other hand. Yet, in 1861, America had a more immediate problem than foreign relations: reuniting the once United States as it split in half over the question of slavery and succession. America now had dual foreign policies, as both the North (anti-slavery) and South (pro-slavery) sections of the country reached out to Europe for help in their cause. This Civil War represented a low ebb in this nation's evolving foreign policy as America turned inward to settle its home strife. Yet, paradoxically, the war had a significant influence on U.S. relations with the world. The firepower and battlefield skill displayed by the North and the South during the war sent a message around the globe that the United States was now a mature military power with legitimate claims of global eminence. When the dust settled on this wrenching, blood-drenched civil war, America returned again to its perceived destiny of westward expansion.

Emergence as a great power, 1898–1920

Events in Cuba would plunge the United States into world affairs in 1898, as the Spanish-American War erupted. This skirmish marked the beginning of concern in Washington over questions of global human rights, resulting from sympathy among U.S. citizens for the plight of destitute Cubans living under the heavy hand of Spanish rule. It was a watershed year in the evolution of U.S. foreign policy. When a mysterious explosion sank the U.S. battleship *Maine* in the Havana harbor, lost beneath the waves, too, were the hopes of the McKinley Administration (1897–1901) for a quick diplomatic settlement with Spain. Public opinion across the United States clamored for revenge. "Remember the *Maine!*" became a potent political slogan that President William McKinley could ill afford to ignore.

America as a colonial power

Congress declared war in April and the U.S. military moved rapidly to subdue the Spanish army in Cuba. Among the spoils of war, the McKinley Administration stripped from Madrid's possession the nearby island of Puerto Rico and the faraway Philippine Islands. With these acquisitions, the United States became a colonial power with interests stretching across the Pacific Ocean, along with a world-class military establishment prepared to defend its new territories. America had arrived on the world stage. It had also adopted an inspiring new cause that would figure more prominently in America's future foreign policy pursuits than any other theme: the promotion of democratic governments around the world. The interest of the United States in the Far East was not fueled alone by its nascent ties to the Philippines and economic considerations; the concern for human rights that had surfaced during the Spanish-American War proved to have strong legs.

American foreign policy was now shot through with a new strain of idealism that sought to carry home-grown concepts of freedom and civil liberties to other parts of the globe. Nonetheless, this sense of idealism had to share a place in Washington with the more muscular viewpoint of the realists. The favorite expression of President Theodore "Teddy" Roosevelt (1901–1909), a hero in the Spanish-American War, was the West African proverb, "Speak softly and carry a big stick." This philosophy morphed into the slogan of "big-stick diplomacy": brandishing the military instrument of foreign policy to persuade overseas adversaries to accept America's demands. This "gunboat diplomacy" was periodically coupled in Washington with "dollar diplomacy" – an approach favored by Roosevelt's successor, William Howard Taft (1909–1913), in which the objective was the exercise of unbridled government support for U.S. corporate interests in Latin American and elsewhere. Military muscle and corporate money, with the additional interest of religious proselytizing on behalf of Christianity and the advancement of democracy and human rights – here were the driving forces behind America's foreign policy at the dawn of the twentieth century.

Wilsonian idealism

With the advent of the Wilson Administration (1913–1921), the United States perpetuated its tradition of keeping at arm's-length from the roiling events of Europe. Isolationism, the dream of turning the clock back to a happier, more peaceful era when America could concentrate on its internal development and westward expansion, again became the order of the day. President Woodrow Wilson, however much he expressed idealist sentiments, did not allow this introspection to weaken the hold of the United States over its self-proclaimed sphere of influence in Latin America. The otherwise dovish president ordered military expeditions into Mexico in 1914, and again in 1916, demonstrating how the United States would continue to assume the posture of a hegemonic guardian when it came to its "own" Western Hemisphere.

In 1916, President Wilson renewed his pledge to keep the United States far removed from war-ravaged Europe. Soon thereafter, though, the Germans began to engage in unrestricted submarine warfare against any ship entering the Atlantic Ocean, including those flying an American flag. Adding to the insult, German Foreign Secretary Arthur Zimmermann sent a secret telegram to his envoy in Mexico, which was intercepted by British naval intelligence and passed along to Washington officials. The telegram ordered the envoy to seek a pact of aggression with Mexico against the United States, should the Americans enter the war against Germany. The payoff would be a return of Texas, New Mexico, and Arizona to the Mexicans. Disclosure of the Zimmermann telegram by the American press was equivalent to throwing kerosene onto the flames of anti-German sentiment within the United States.

The increasingly bellicose behavior of the Germans was too much even for the irenic Wilson to bear. He urged war against Germany in a speech before Congress on April 2, 1917, and when the lawmakers obliged with a declaration of war, the president sent two million American soldiers overseas to help tip the scales against the Kaiser. In Wilson's words, America's soldiers would fight to make the world "safe for democracy," in a "final war for human liberty." After the death of six million soldiers, including 116,516 in American uniform, the conflict was finally ended on November 11, 1918. President Wilson turned to what had become his number one objective: the daunting task of preventing all future wars through the establishment of a League of Nations. In an exhausting series of speeches across the United States that would break his health and lead to a severe stroke, Wilson presented to the public the merits of the League. The Senate remained unimpressed, however, and amended Wilson's proposal beyond recognition. Disgusted by the sweeping revisions, the president withdrew support for the transfigured document and the Senate buried his beloved treaty proposal.

In the end, several major nations embraced the League (at least on paper); but the United States refused to become a member, even though America's own president had put forth the initiative. Democrats continued to cling to the idea of a League; but, echoing the Senate's position against foreign involvement, a majority of the voters turned against the Democratic Party in the presidential election of 1920 and voted for the Republican candidate Warren G. Harding (1921–1923), who promised a return to "normalcy." In the constitutional system of divided institutions sharing power, the legislative branch had won out and appeared to be more in tune with the isolationist sentiments of the American people.

America as a reluctant leader, 1921–1945

The Great Depression began in 1929 and turned the United States even further inward, as the American people attempted to cope with the nation's most severe unemployment and financial dislocation ever. Overseas, only Latin America received much attention from the highest levels of the government, as President Franklin D. Roosevelt (1933–1945) removed all U.S. troops south of the Rio Grande, with the exception of those stationed in the Panama Canal Zone, and proclaimed a new "good neighbor policy" toward Latin America.

The fascist and communist threats

On the heels of the Great Depression, the United States was rudely awakened from its isolationist stance by the greatest challenges Americans had faced from abroad since the early wars against Great Britain: the rise of fascism and communism, twin threats that would dominate international affairs for the greater part of the twentieth century. The League of Nations proved too feeble to halt the aggression; and critics were quick to blame the absence of the United States from the League's membership as the chief cause of its failure. Yet no nation – member of the League or not – did anything to reverse the Japanese military advances in Asia. This passivity in the West set a match to the parchments on which the League had been written. An admiring and opportunistic witness to the ease with which Japan took over Manchuria and Shanghai, Italy's Benito Mussolini sent his military into Ethiopia in 1936 and joined a fascist alliance with Adolf Hitler of Germany. Japan allied itself with these Axis powers in the same year and turned toward its major objective in 1937, the conquest of China.

Still the United States and the rest of the world did nothing, looking away as the Japanese massacred the Chinese people on a grand scale. Americans and their leaders did not like what was happening, but they disliked even more the notion of involving their own flesh and blood in costly combat on a distant continent. Disillusioned by the First World War, viewed by many Americans as an unfortunate involvement by the United States in Europe's petty bickering, isolationists tried to avoid the same mistake again.

Adolf Hitler ordered German troops to occupy Austria in 1938, and then seized a part of Czechoslovakia. Again, America, Great Britain, Russia, and France stood by passively. British Prime Minister Neville Chamberlain finally led a diplomatic rescue attempt, meeting in Munich with Hitler. The leaders signed a document that proclaimed, "the desire of our two peoples never to go to war with one another again." Six months later Nazi tanks occupied the rest of Czechoslovakia. Munich, the site of the Chamberlain meeting with Hitler, became a location forever synonymous with the idea of "appeasement" – the futility of attempting to satiate fanatics by yielding to their demands. A policy of appeasement came to mean a leader's lack of spine in the conduct of foreign affairs.

On September 1, 1939, German Panzer tanks next crushed the brave but poorly armed Polish resistance, many of whom rode into battle on horseback. The British and the French honored their defense treaty with Poland and declared war against the Nazis. The Second World War had begun. Despite these chilling events in Europe, isolationist opinions remained strong among Americans. President Roosevelt repeatedly vowed that the United States would remain neutral. A series of disheartening Nazi military successes, however, gave him a new perspective on the potential dangers facing the United States. Although the American people were still unwilling to enter into war, the president began to take steps toward aiding the British. "We must be the great arsenal of democracy," he declared as 1940 came to a close, adding that the United States would support the Allied Powers "by all means short of war."

The president proposed that the United States supply military weaponry to the United Kingdom. As he explained to the American public, the United States was reacting like someone who would lend a garden hose to a neighbor whose house was on fire. This persuasive metaphor notwithstanding, isolationists in Congress opposed the measure. Undaunted, using an executive order (an e.o., rather than legislation), Roosevelt came to the aid of the British in September of 1940 by providing them with 50 aging U.S. destroyers in exchange for American naval base rights in British-owned Bermuda. Further, he introduced conscription (a military draft), implemented again by way of an executive order. Both actions signaled an end to neutrality. These initiatives inflamed isolationists on Capitol Hill. "We have torn up 150 years of traditional foreign policy," opined their leader in Congress, Senator Arthur H. Vandenberg (R-Michigan). "We have tossed [President George] Washington's Farewell Address [which had cautioned against 'entangling alliances'] into the discard." Nevertheless, a larger number of other lawmakers voted to fund Roosevelt's Lend Lease Act in March 1941, which allowed the president to supply the British with tanks, aircraft, ammunition, and food for the war effort.

Then came December 7, 1941, and the Japanese attack on Pearl Harbor – a day that, in Roosevelt's enduring words, would "live in infamy." America's insistence that the Japanese withdraw from China, coupled with a U.S. ban against the sale of aviation fuel and scrap metal to Japan, angered officials in Tokyo and led to the surprise Japanese bombing at Hawaii, an American territory at the time. With this turn of events, even the staunchest isolationists in Congress were ready to fight. "The only thing now to do is lick hell of out them," declared one of their prominent spokesmen, Senator Burton K. Wheeler (D-Montana).

Embracing internationalism ... gingerly

Four years of global warfare that had sent 60 million people to premature graves and left much of Europe, Russia, and Japan in a wrecked heap finally ended in 1945, in a victory for the United States and its allies in Europe and the Pacific. The war ushered in the nuclear age with America's bombing of Hiroshima and Nagasaki, which revealed how atomic weapons could destroy whole cities in an instant. The war led as well to a new era of international cooperation, in which the United States was the acknowledged leader. In a revival of Wilsonism spurred by the horrors of the war, most of the world's countries gathered in San Francisco in July 1945 to establish a United Nations, the most ambitious experiment in international organization ever tried. From the beginning, though, the UN exhibited a fatal weakness. Just as with the League of Nations, it had no workable international police force to halt military aggression by rogue nations. Still, hopes remained high among liberal internationalists that the creation of the UN would be an important step toward Wilson's dream of a lasting world peace.

World peace, though, remained a distant dream. No sooner had the United States demobilized its troops after the victory over fascism than yet a new threat emerged on the horizon: a "Cold War" between the Western democracies and the Moscow-led communist nations of the world. The leader of Russia's "Soviet Union," Joseph Stalin – an erstwhile ally with the United States against the Nazis – had become increasingly truculent toward the United States. He was, as well, highly aggressive in his rhetoric about communist expansion around the globe, not to mention being shockingly cruel to his own people and domineering over contiguous nations.

In 1946, former British Prime Minister Winston Churchill described the new world in a speech at Westminster College in Fulton, Missouri: "From Stettin in the Baltic to Trieste in the Adriatic, an iron curtain has descended across the continent ... all these famous cities and the populations around them lie in the Soviet sphere and all are subject in one form or another, not only to Soviet influence but a very high and increasing measure of control from Moscow." Every president throughout the Cold War, from Truman to George H. W. Bush, would place the Soviet Union at the top of their lists of foreign policy threats to the United States – and rightly so since the Soviets had acquired the capacity to strike North America with atomic warheads delivered by bombers as early as 1950 and, soon thereafter, by swift intercontinental ballistic missiles (ICBMs). In the chilling and all too accurate acronym of the era, each of the two "superpowers" had the capacity to retaliate against an attack with a massive counterpunch: a condition known as mutual assured destruction or MAD, with its rain of nuclear bombs that would leave each civilization in radioactive ruins.

After the war, the United States moved dramatically away from its long-held isolationist leanings toward a posture of greater global involvement. As a result of rapidly expanding U.S. commercial ventures, one could purchase a Coke in the heart of Africa or stay in a Holiday Inn while traveling in northwestern China. Nonetheless, many Americans remained ambivalent about foreign entanglements, fearful that the resources of the United States might again be diverted away from pressing needs at home. The responses of the American people to these expectations of global leadership during and after the Cold War have resulted in both foreign policy successes and failures, as the next two chapters relate.

Notes

On the emergence of the United States as a significant world power, see: Thomas A. Bailey, *A Diplomatic History of the American People*, 9th ed. (Englewood Cliffs, NJ: Prentice Hall, 1974); Hollis W. Barber, *Foreign Policies of the United States* (New York: Dryden, 1953); John Lewis Gaddis, *Surprise, Security, and the American Experience* (Cambridge, MA: Harvard University Press, 2004); Ernest R. May, *Imperial Democracy: The Emergence of America as a Great Power* (New York: Harcourt, Brace & World, 1961); and Dexter Perkins, *The Evolution of American Foreign Policy* (New York: Oxford University Press, 1948). Also: Gary A. Donaldson, *American Foreign Policy: The Twentieth Century in Documents* (New York: Longman, 2003); Daniel S. Papp, Loch K. Johnson, and John E. Endicott, *American Foreign Policy: History, Politics, and Policy* (New York: Pearson/Longman, 2005); and Gaddis Smith, "The Legacy of Monroe's Doctrine," *New York Times Magazine* (September 9, 1984): 44–48.

4   Cold War

From the beginning of the Cold War in 1946 to its ending in 1991, the United States had to cope with a world more complicated and dangerous than ever before. The United States was now a major world power. Moreover, the era of nuclear weapons held out the prospect that a regional war could spread to engulf the superpowers, leading to the extinction of the human race. In psychologist Erik Erikson's chilling assessment, Homo sapiens had become "a species mortally dangerous to itself."

Several events were important in defining international affairs during the Cold War, beyond the invention of nuclear weapons with their massive powers of instant destruction. Among them: the emergence of the United States and the Soviet Union as superpowers and the global confrontation between these two nations – the essence of what we mean by the "Cold War"; the splintering of the world into almost 200 nations, as the old colonial empires disintegrated; and, finally, the collapse of the Soviet empire at the end of this period. The Cold War was a time of significant risk for the United States. For these 45 years, Americans faced an adversary capable of reducing America's cities into a pile of rubble – the same condition that would have visited the Soviet Union when the United States returned fire. In the famous analogy of nuclear scientist J. Robert Oppenheimer, the superpowers were like "two scorpions in a bottle," fearful of attacking one another because the end result would be death for both.

The containment doctrine

Unlike the USSR, the United States demobilized its troops after the war, as Americans again sought to remove themselves from the world. These isolationist sentiments were not as extreme as they had been in the aftermath of the First World War; nonetheless, Americans were now going to concentrate on priorities at home. Meanwhile, Soviet leaders consolidated their control over the nations of Eastern Europe, as well as Mongolia, by forcing these once free countries to become Moscow's satellites. Attacked too often in the past by armies from Europe, and with the loss of twenty-six million soldiers and civilians in the Second World War (almost 15 percent of the Soviet population), leaders in the Kremlin viewed their conquests-by-intimidation in Eastern Europe as a vital step toward the establishment of a buffer zone against future threats from abroad.

For Western Europeans and their American allies, however, this projection of Soviet power – accompanied by rhetoric from Moscow boasting that the Marxist-Leninist way of life would soon overshadow democracy and capitalism – represented an unsettling turn of events. The true intentions of the Soviets were largely a matter of speculation; but the brutal hand of Russian suppression over Eastern Europe, along with the manner in which the brusque leader of the Soviet Union, Joseph Stalin, broke one treaty promise after another with the United States and other nations, indicated to the West that an erstwhile friend had become a foreboding adversary. The Soviet leader's attacks against the West were more than rhetorical. The USSR was involved in the widespread use of covert actions to undermine free elections in Italy, France, and West Germany, beginning in 1946, while at the same time they secretly funded the communist parties in these nations and many others.

"I do not think we should play compromise any longer," President Truman told his Secretary of State, Dean Acheson. "I'm tired of babying the Soviets." No other nation in the West could stand up to the Soviets. The United Kingdom and the European continental powers had been devastated by the war, their far-flung colonial empires in a state of financial ruin, their armies shattered.

Soon to be one of the most influential voices in American foreign policy was a young U.S. diplomat stationed in Moscow by the name of George F. Kennan, author of what would become the containment doctrine, America's grand strategy for dealing with the Soviets. "At the bottom of the Kremlin's neurotic view of world affairs," he wrote in an article published by *Foreign Affairs* (anonymously signed as "X"), "is the traditional and instinctive Russian sense of insecurity." To counter Soviet aggressiveness, Kennan recommend in a key passage: "... a long-term, patient but firm and vigilant containment of Russian expansive tendencies." This strategy of patience and firmness, with what soon became an emphasis on the latter in the Truman and Eisenhower Administrations, was initially most evident in what became known as the Truman Doctrine: President Truman's proclamation of a Greek-Turkish foreign aid package in March of 1947. As Truman told Congress, it would be the policy of the United States "to support free people who are resisting attempted subjugation by armed minorities or by outside pressures." The phrase "armed minorities" was a reference to communist insurgents around the world financed by the Kremlin (the "outside pressures").

Kennan had advocated neither the use of military force to contain communism, except as a final resort, nor resistance to communism everywhere in the world. In the first instance, he believed that the United States could successfully employ political, economic, and, especially, psychological pressures on the Soviets to change their behavior. As historian John Lewis Gaddis writes, "the very purpose of 'containment' had been to change the *psychology* of the Soviet leadership." Toward this end, Kennan urged the United States to align itself with the strongest of all anti-communist forces on the globe: nationalism.

A new militancy

The United States continued to feel, on the one hand, the tug of isolationists who wished to retreat from the entanglements of external relations, yet, on the other hand, the counter-tug of internationalists who argued for U.S. global leadership against the new threat to world peace presented by the Soviet Union. The isolationists worried about the costs of America's new role in the world, as foreign nations lined up for U.S. assistance. "Don't be Santa Claus!" was a popular isolationist slogan. Most Americans supported the idea of containment; but officials in Washington, backed by lobbyists for the burgeoning military-industrial complex, interpreted Kennan's more nuanced prescriptions as a call to arms. "The Cold War became an arms race, exactly what Kennan had hoped to prevent," remarks Louis Menand. Cold War historian Gaddis adds: "Trapped in their own rhetoric, leaders of the United States found it difficult to respond to the conciliatory gestures which emanated from the

Kremlin following Stalin's death and, through their inflexibility, may well have contributed to the perpetuation of the cold war."

The communist takeover in Czechoslovakia (1948); the Berlin blockade (1948); the loss of China to communists in a civil war that drove the anti-communist Chinese offshore to Taiwan (1949); the successful Soviet testing of a nuclear bomb (1949), several years ahead of the CIA's estimated date; and, a major turning point, the war in Korea (1950–1953), would convert most of the isolationists into supporters of the us-versus-them Cold War stance taken by the Truman Administration and its successors. These international events led most initial doubters to embrace Truman's more militant responses to the Soviet threat over Kennan's softer reliance on diplomacy, trade, and propaganda.

The red-baiting at the height of the McCarthy era (1952–1954), when Senator Joseph McCarthy (R-Wisconsin) made a national reputation by blaming, with flimsy evidence, the nation's foreign policy woes on unnamed phantom communists engaged in treason within the U.S. government, had a further stifling effect on those who might have questioned the bellicose form the containment doctrine had assumed. McCarthy was correct to an extent: there were some communists who had infiltrated the federal government, including the high-level British spy Klaus Fuchs in the Manhattan Project; but the senator's unfair tactics of smear and innuendo, along with his overreach – "McCarthyism," as this over-the-top, slanted approach came to be known – eventually discredited him and his allegations.

By 1950, the Truman Administration was prepared to state in its most important decision document on national security, the National Security Council Paper No. 68 or simply NSC-68, that "the assault on free institutions is worldwide now, and in the context of the present polarization of power a defeat of free institutions anywhere is a defeat everywhere." The Cold War had turned into a zero-sum game in which any communist gain was seen as an American loss. All Marxist, communist, and even many socialist nations in the developing world, regardless of how small their strategic importance or how weak their allegiance to Moscow, were now considered enemies of the United States.

Subsequently, the Eisenhower Administration (1953–1961) preached the same gospel, only with more fire and brimstone. President Dwight D.

Eisenhower's Secretary of State, John Foster Dulles, warned that "already one-third of the world is dominated by an imperialist brand of communism; already the free world has been so shrunk that no further substantial parts of it can be lost without danger to the whole that remains." Neither the Truman nor the Eisenhower Administrations carried out these pronouncements to the point of initiating open warfare against the Soviet Union, with all the dire consequences that might have brought. Dulles often spoke with passion about the "liberation" of the Soviet satellite states in Eastern Europe; however, as Gaddis has noted, this posturing was motivated "more by determination to lure East European voting blocs [in the United States] away from the Democrats than from any realistic expectations of 'rolling back' Moscow's sphere of influence."

Peril points

A concern in Washington was that, out of sheer exhaustion and disillusionment, the governments of Europe would simply buckle under pressure from the Soviet Union. The United States moved to strengthen the European economy through the infusion of billions of dollars in economic aid – a policy known as the Marshall Plan or, more formally, the European Recovery Program (ERP). Named after Secretary of State George C. Marshall, who had served with distinction as army chief of staff during the war, this program of assistance was designed to strengthen the sagging economies of Europe, thus making them resistant to communist influence.

Then, in 1949, the United States joined with Canada and Western Europe in the creation of America's first peacetime military alliance since the early days of the Republic. Labeled the North Atlantic Treaty Organization (NATO), this pact committed the United States to the placement of soldiers in Europe on a permanent basis. The combined forces of NATO would provide the muscle to protect and advance economic recovery in Europe. In 1953, the Soviet Union responded by forming a Moscow-led security alliance of its own, known as the Warsaw Pact, comprised of the Soviet Union and the nations of Eastern Europe.

The Korean War

The most extreme outward probes by the communists came not in Europe, however, but first in Asia and then in America's own backyard. Korea had become a divided nation. The government in the north was a Soviet and Chinese satellite, while the government in the south was recognized by the UN and supported by the United States. In June of 1950, the Soviet- and Chinese-backed army of the Democratic People's Republic of Korea suddenly advanced into South Korea. Though geographically distant from the United States, the Korean peninsula was seen as a possible strategic stepping stone for the communists toward Japan, a nation of strategic importance in the struggle to protect the free and open societies against the authoritarian regimes.

Moreover, Korea had taken on added significance in light of President Truman's vow that no nation was too remote in America's struggle against global communism. The United States, leading a UN coalition, entered the war of South Korea against the North Korean communists. This contest was important because of the opportunity it presented for a display of Western, chiefly American, determination to resist the global spread of communism. After three years of intense fighting that cost the lives of over 35,000 U.S. troops, the war ended in a stalemate. The war had been unpopular at home; but it did achieve the tangible effect of forcing the communists to retreat behind the 38th parallel, the demilitarized zone (DMZ) that bisected the Korean peninsula at the time (and still does). The Western nations had demonstrated to the dictators in Russia, China, and North Korea that the spread of communism would be fiercely resisted.

Crises in Cuba

The Administration of John F. Kennedy (1961–1963) carried on President Eisenhower's planning to overthrow the Cuban president, Fidel Castro. In 1961, the CIA landed a team of Cuban exiles on the island's beaches at the Bay of Pigs. The operations side of the Agency anticipated that the people of Cuba would greet the "liberators" with open arms and join them in a counter-revolution. In reality, however, most Cubans remained loyal to Castro, whose soldiers easily defeated the small paramilitary force. Then, in the next year, the Soviets forced the United States into the most perilous confrontation that occurred between the superpowers during the Cold War: the Cuban missile crisis. Soviet leader Nikita Khrushchev ordered the placement of Soviet nuclear missiles on Cuban soil during October of 1962. Some advisers, including Secretary of Defense Robert S. McNamara, argued that no U.S. military response was necessary, because Americans already lived under the shadow of Soviet strategic missiles, including some close by on submarines in the Atlantic Ocean. Others argued for a diplomatic settlement, perhaps swapping U.S. missiles in Turkey for the Soviet missiles in Cuba; and some participants in military uniform were spoiling for a fight with the Cuban dictator.

As the tense two weeks of the crisis flew by, President Kennedy leaned toward a decision that combined a show of strength and determination with a measure of prudence. The United States established a "quarantine" around Cuba to keep out further shipments of Soviet missiles to the island. The question was whether the Soviets would turn back their missile-laden freighters, or perhaps use their submarines armed with nuclear warheads to punch a hole through the blockade. A sense of crisis spread across the United States, but good news came at last on October 28: Khrushchev had decided to turn back all the Soviet freighters and dismantle the missiles under construction in Cuba. The Kremlin had stepped away from the abyss. A back-channel deal on trading the missiles in Turkey for the Cuban missiles had its desired effect. In addition, the Soviet leader probably found sobering the fact that the United States enjoyed a 5,000-to-300 advantage in ICBMs at the time. Nevertheless, the superpowers had edged close to the rim of Armageddon.

Vietnam

By 1963, the Kennedy Administration found itself deeply embroiled in the political machinations of internal South Vietnamese politics, even condoning a military coup against President Ngo Dinh Diem, who was murdered along with his brother by rival South Vietnamese generals friendly toward the United States. At the time of President Kennedy's own death in November of 1963, the number of U.S. military advisers in South Vietnam had swollen to some 16,500. Passed along to the next president, Lyndon B. Johnson (1963–1969), the conflict would become a Bay of Pigs in slow motion.

President Johnson began an escalation of the conflict in Vietnam, both in rhetoric and in the number of U.S. troops sent to that battlefield. What was at first supposed to be a limited operation meant to shield American military advisers and warships in that region soon became, in the president's speeches, a fundamental test of America's will to halt communist expansion in Southeast Asia. The small number of American soldiers initially sent to South Vietnam under Johnson in 1963–1964 were joined in the spring of 1965 – without public knowledge or congressional debate – by thousands more, rising to a total of over 128,000 by the end of the year. The war went badly for the United States. The U.S. military found the jungle terrain alien and, further, "irregular" guerrilla warfare was still something of a novelty for Americans –not at all like the head-on clashes and distinguishable fronts of the Second World War and the Korean conflict.

For the next eight years, until 1973, the fighting in Vietnam went on. Over 57,000 Americans lost their lives. Fearful that dramatic escalation might bring in Chinese or even Soviet armies, yet unwilling to retreat and incur the political wrath of those who would blame the Democrats for being soft on communism, the Johnson Administration opted for a middle course. The end result was a bloody war of attrition that led first to a stalemate (as occurred in the Korean War) and then a slide toward outright defeat, with a steady stream of dead American soldiers shipped home in pine boxes, often under the cover of darkness to avoid media reporting on the numbers who had perished.

Accompanying these horrific losses came a growing public alienation toward the war in Indochina. Every evening, television news in the United States carried gruesome images of death and destruction in Vietnam: burning villages engulfed in napalm; wounded GIs evacuated by helicopter, their faces contorted in pain; rag-doll figures of men, women, and children massacred at the village of My Lai – a mass murder of Vietnamese civilians by overzealous American soldiers; the profusion of bomb craters that became the pockmarks of the distress that had infected Vietnam; the chaos of Saigon, with the bodies of protesting Buddhist monks aflame in self-emulations. On television, too, came the seemingly incessant count of American soldiers killed each week, along with U.S. Army generals speaking of victory just around the corner – with always another corner. And demonstrations on the college campuses and streets of America that often erupted into violent clashes with police and members of the National Guard in various states, with the Ohio Guard shooting dead four students at Kent State University in 1970, along with two more students killed by police at Jackson State University in Mississippi.

Opposition from within his own party, coupled with Johnson's decline in the public opinion polls, led to an unexpected political decision on March 31, 1968. In a stunning television address to the nation, the president announced that he would not seek a second term. Hubert H. Humphrey, vice president in the Johnson Administration, went on to capture the Democratic Party nomination as antiwar protesters – mainly college students from around the country – clashed violently with police in the streets of Chicago outside the meeting arena of the national nominating convention. The Republican nominee, Richard M. Nixon, narrowly won the general election, in large part because Humphrey had supported the failing war in Vietnam. Rarely had foreign policy played such an important role in the outcome of a presidential election. Prominent in Nixon's campaign rhetoric was a promise to end the war in Vietnam. The negotiations between his top foreign policy aide, Secretary of State Henry Kissinger, and the North Vietnamese failed. So did the ongoing American bombing of Hanoi and other cities in North Vietnam, as well as a controversial U.S. invasion of Cambodia in May of 1970 to close down this enemy sanctuary – again without any congressional debate or approval.

While President Nixon wrestled with how to end the war – a period during which an additional 20,000 died in Vietnam – he was caught up in the Watergate scandal. Newspaper reporting in *The Washington Post* disclosed the president's attempt to cover up criminal evidence that implicated his White House aides in a burglary of the Democratic Party's national headquarters offices in the Watergate Hotel in Washington. Members of Congress investigated the allegations and, in August of 1974, Nixon resigned in the face of a seemingly inevitable impeachment conviction in the Senate. The final retreat from Vietnam fell to his vice president and successor, Gerald R. Ford (1974–1977), a former member of the House of Representatives from Michigan. In April of 1975, North Vietnamese troops surrounded South Vietnam's capital, Saigon. Kennan later referred to this war as "the most disastrous of all America's undertakings over the whole 200 years of its history."

Détente

The Vietnam experience also called into question the most fundamental tenet of American foreign policy during the Cold War: the containment doctrine. Observing a widening of the schism between China and the Soviet Union, which had begun to yawn in 1962, Nixon and Kissinger set out to prod China farther away from Moscow's influence, a policy known as the "opening to China." Further, America's icy relations with the USSR underwent a remarkable thaw during the Nixon years, an ironic outcome since Nixon had built his political reputation as a devoted Soviet-basher. Nudged in this more diplomatic direction by Kissinger (again, ironically, because he had been an unreconstructed Cold Warrior), President Nixon ushered in a period of relaxed tensions between the superpowers, known as détente and punctuated by arms control accords and increased trade agreements between the superpowers.

The Cold War revived

Under President Ronald Reagan (1981–1989), the Cold War took on new life. The Soviet Union was an "evil empire," he declared. Covert actions by the CIA proliferated around the world. This Reagan Doctrine, less a formal policy statement than an appellation applied by the media to the Administration's new aggressiveness toward the Soviets, envisaged the robust use of secret operations to assist other nations in their resistance to communist influence. Then, unpredictably, during the final years of the Reagan Administration and throughout the following Administration led by George H. W. Bush (1989–1993), the world witnessed breakthrough efforts in both Washington and Moscow to ease – and then erase – the Cold War.

Notes

On the beginnings of the Cold War, see John Lewis Gaddis, *The United States and the Origins of the Cold War: 1941–1947* (New York: Columbia

University Press, 1972). For Kennan's containment doctrine article, see X, "The Sources of Soviet Conduct," *Foreign Affairs* 25 (July 1947): 566–582. Helpful overviews of the Cold War can be found in Richard J. Barnet, *Real Security: Restoring American Power in a Dangerous Decade* (New York: Simon & Schuster, 1981); Leslie H. Gelb and Richard K. Betts, *The Irony of Vietnam: The System Worked* (Washington, D.C.: Brookings Institution, 1979); Louis Menand, "Getting Real: George F. Kennan's Cold War," *The New Yorker* (November 14, 2011): 84–87; Richard H. Rovere, *Senator Joe McCarthy* (Berkeley: University of California Press, 1959); and Thomas C. Schelling, *Arms and Influence* (New Haven, CT: Yale University Press, 1966). The Dulles quote is from John Lewis Gaddis, *Strategies of Containment* (New York: Oxford University Press, 1982): 130–131; and the Erikson quote is from Robert C. Tucker, *Politics as Leadership* (Columbia: University of Missouri Press, 1981): x.

5 American foreign policy in a fractious world

Foreign policy in flux

The startling collapse of the Soviet Union as a global superpower in 1990–1991 altered the nature of world politics. Throughout the Cold War, the USSR had been Priority No. 1 in the containment calculations of Washington's foreign policy officials. With the disappearance of the Soviet empire, the focus of American foreign policy shifted and broadened. As R. James Woolsey, a Director of Central Intelligence (DCI), put it: the Soviet dragon had been slain, but the United States now confronted "a jungle filled with a bewildering variety of poisonous snakes."

Ethnic and tribal disputes suddenly flared into violence around the globe. In Yugoslavia, unrest burst into a full-blown civil war that ripped asunder the loosely threaded seams that once held this nation together under the threat of Soviet intervention. In Africa, tribal warfare in Somalia grew more intense, with hundreds of civilians caught in the crossfire and thousands more starving to death as drought continued to plague the land and tribal bandits persisted in their theft of food from international relief agencies. In January 1993, Czechoslovakia snapped in two – peacefully at least – along an ethnic fissure, creating separate Czech and Slovak republics. The trash bins of harried cartographers filled with outdated drawings of national boundaries that seemed to shift from month to month.

A new world disorder

The Administration of George H. W. Bush was understandably elated when the Soviet Union collapsed during its watch. The president spoke of a New World Order, a time of global peace that would replace the strife that had darkened the era of the Cold War. Yet, proclamations from the White House notwithstanding, the world had become anything but orderly; rather, a new world *disorder* seemed to take the place of the previous superpower stand-off. The United States found itself engaged in wars for the first time in the volatile Muslim regions of the Middle East and Southwest Asia; and, by 1998, the specter of global terrorism had cast a disquieting shadow across Americans at home and abroad.

The most spectacular world event in the years since 1945 was a second Russian revolution. The first, in 1917, brought communism to power; the second, in 1989–1991, saw the internal overthrow of the Soviet Union. In 1985, President Mikhail S. Gorbachev came to power in Moscow. He understood that the Marxist-Leninist experiment of a state-controlled society had failed. In place of state repression, he established a new system that had some attributes of democracy and a market economy. The transition was, observed Kennan, "a turning point of the most momentous historical significance." Among the 15 newly free nations that had once comprised the Soviet Union, Lithuania became the first to request admission to NATO in 1994; Estonia and Latvia soon followed suit. In 1996, NATO decided to expand eastward and admitted into its membership the Czech Republic, Hungary, and Poland, along with the Baltic nations – in each case over the strong protest of leaders in the Kremlin. Most of the nuclear warheads in the former Soviet republics remained intact, as well as vast numbers of sophisticated conventional weaponry. At least, though, the United States and Russia co-signed the Strategic Arms Reduction Talks (START) Treaty II, authorizing cutbacks in the number of strategic nuclear warheads in both nations by some two-thirds.

Vladimir Putin, a former member of the Soviet foreign intelligence agency (the KGB), became Russia's president in 2000 and tightened centralized political and economic control in Moscow, banishing Gorbachev to the sidelines. Presidents George W. Bush and Putin signed another important arms agreement, the Strategic Offensive Arms Reduction Treaty, in 2002 that cut U.S. and Soviet strategic nuclear arsenals to the lowest total in decades, at about 2,000 warheads each. In 2010, Washington and Moscow also endorsed a "New Start" Treaty to strengthen arms-control verification measures and continue a phased reduction of nuclear weapons. Despite these useful arms accords, events inside Russia were worrisome as under Putin they slipped further away from the moorings of democratic reform.

Desert Storm

In 1991, President Bush I decided to repel, with a massive U.S.-led military force, an Iraqi invasion into neighboring Kuwait, a small oil-rich regime on the Persian Gulf. Known as "Operation Desert Storm," America's First Persian Gulf War was a bold manifestation of the president's hope to maintain some semblance of a New World Order. Over 100,000 Iraqi soldiers died in battle, compared with 137 American troops (one-fourth of whom were accidentally killed by friendly fire). It was the most lop-sided victory in the annals of modern warfare, a result of superior U.S. firepower and intelligence-gathering capabilities (including sophisticated satellite photographs of the battlefields in Iraq). The success raised the president's popularity at home to above the 90th percentile in surveys on "presidential job approval" – the highest point ever recorded.

Also in 1991, President Bush signed National Security Review No. 29 (NSR-29), which directed America's secret agencies to compile the most exhaustive list of intelligence priorities since the end of the Second World War. At the top of the list was concern about the dangerous proliferation of WMD around the world. Terrorism was on the list, too, but without any special sense of urgency. The United States would soon find out that here was the greatest immediate danger to Americans.

Bloodbath in the Balkans

Crowding the foreign policy agenda of the Clinton Administration (1993–2001) was the disintegration of Yugoslavia and a civil war that raged across its former parts, especially in the heartland of Bosnia-Herzegovina and Serbia. Nowhere was the post-Cold War revival of atavistic ethnic grievances more apparent. Inside the boundaries of what was, until 1990, a sovereign state dwelled people of Albanian, Bulgarian, Croat, Hungarian, Macedonian, Montenegrin, Muslim, Serb, Slovak, and Slovene descent. During the Cold War, their animosities had been held in check by the fear that Soviet tanks would intervene across the border if unrest broke out. Now that check had vanished.

"Barbarism" is not too strong a word when one examines this civil war. From its inception in 1991, triggered by the desire of Serbian leaders to create in the place of Yugoslavia a "Greater Serbia," reports of atrocities poured out of the region on an almost daily basis, including over 20,000 rapes of Muslim women by Serbian soldiers. The Serbs also engaged in mass murders, including over 200 hospitalized Croats who were taken from their beds in 1992 and shot point-blank in a nearby field. Each of the ethnic groups involved in the conflict violated accepted canons of modern warfare. In 1992, for example, Bosnian Muslims killed over 60 Serbs, chiefly civilians, in villages near the town of Bratunac. Here was the New World Order. Unilateral intervention by the United States with ground troops was an option firmly rejected by the Clinton Administration. As 1995 came to a close, however, the United States managed to broker the Dayton Peace Accords among Croats, Bosnian Muslims, and Serbs. The talks resulted in a division of Yugoslavia along ethnic lines. The United Nations ended its deployment in the Balkans and NATO took over the job of enforcing the Dayton Accords. Fighter aircraft and bombers flown by NATO pilots filled the skies above the battlefields and this region of the Balkans began to enjoy peace, however tenuous.

Chaos in Somalia

In 1992, the United States sent troops into Somalia to provide protection for UN humanitarian relief efforts – the largest purely humanitarian intervention abroad in America's history, codenamed "Operation Restore Hope." The next year, well-armed Somali warlords killed 18 U.S. Black Hawk helicopter pilots and crew members, in what became known as the Battle of Mogadishu. The firefight, the most intensive since Vietnam, raised important foreign policy questions about the post-Cold War era. Did the concept of a New World Order envision the possibility that anyone with a problem could simply dial 911 and ask for a US-UN-NATO rescue team? How much would it cost the American taxpayer? How much blood of U.S. soldiers would be spilled?

The Clinton Administration faced another test of its diplomatic skills when unrest boiled over in Haiti, sending thousands of refugees in rickety boats toward Florida. The president decided that a U.S. military intervention in Haiti was necessary to stem the flow of refugees and restore order on the poverty-stricken island. "Operation Uphold Democracy" thrust the United States into the role of nation-building, a mission in which it has mostly failed. Haiti remains mired in poverty; but at least some semblance of order returned to the island in 1994, thanks to the presence of U.S. and UN soldiers. America's response to a crisis of genocide in Rwanda in 1994 was less successful. The Clinton Administration vacillated and 800,000 died in tribal warfare before assistance finally arrived from the United States and other nations. Once burned by Somalia, the Administration had been twice shy about entry into further turmoil in Africa. President Clinton later apologized to the people of Rwanda for America's slow response. He admitted that this had been the worst failure of his Administration in the realm of foreign policy.

The rise of global terrorism

Not long after the end of the Cold War, America became the prime target of a new terrorist movement centered in the Afghan-based organization Al Qaeda ("The Base," in Arabic) and led by Osama bin Laden (OBL, for short in CIA lingo). The son of a Saudi construction millionaire, OBL became disaffected with the Western democracies, and the United States in particular, mainly because of their support for Israel, a country seen as an enemy of Islam. The Qaeda objective was to win a global *jihad* ("holy war") against the Western Judeo-Christian "infidels" and establish an Islamic world order or "caliphate."

Signs of terrorist danger long preceded the infamous Qaeda assaults against the American homeland on September 11, 2001, referred to commonly as the 9/11 attacks – or the "day of fire," as President Bush II remembered the attack in his memoirs. As early as 1995, the CIA's Counterterrorism Center (CTC) had cautioned the Clinton White House that U.S. cities could become primary Qaeda targets. According to the CTC, "aerial terrorism seems likely at some point – filling an airplane with explosives and dive-bombing a target." The warning erred only in its failure to understand that hijacked commercial aircraft, with their volatile jet fuel, would be powerful missiles in their own right without added explosives. Yet the CTC was never able to provide Washington officials with precise information about the timing or location of the anticipated hijackings. Such "actionable intelligence" would have given U.S. authorities the ability to intercept the terrorists before they boarded the commercial airliners that they would fly into the World Trade Center and the Pentagon on 9/11.

Despite the CIA's red flag about aerial terrorism, neither the Clinton nor the second Bush Administrations took meaningful steps to tighten airport security, seal off airliner cockpits, field air marshals, or alert top officials in the Department of Transportation (which screened airport passengers) about the possibility of a terrorist operation of this kind. The government's top counterterrorism expert during these years, Richard A. Clarke, recalls warning the new National Security Adviser, Dr. Condoleezza Rice in the second Bush Administration, in January of 2001, about Al Qaeda. He urged her to hold a National Security Council (NSC) meeting on this threat as soon as possible. Rice finally got around to scheduling a session on this topic on September 4, 2001 – by then, too late.

In the aftermath of the 9/11 attacks, the Bush II Administration organized "Operation Enduring Freedom," a counterattack against Al Qaeda in Afghanistan. The Administration targeted, as well, the Taliban regime that had provided a safe haven for the organization throughout the 1990s and during the attacks on the United States in 2001. The counterattack employed an effective mix of CIA paramilitary officers and military Special Forces, supported by B-52 bombers. This combination, aided by the assistance of anti-Taliban tribesmen on the ground in Afghanistan (the Northern Alliance), toppled the government and sent Qaeda members fleeing. Before the United States could round up Bin Laden and his followers, however, they vanished like ghosts into the mountains of Afghanistan and Pakistan. Rather than pursue them, the Administration rashly turned its attention to nearby Iraq, claiming wrongly that its ruler Saddam Hussein had supported the 9/11 attacks, and – again wrongly – that he was constructing WMD for use against the United States.

The Bush Administration authorized individuals captured in Afghanistan and Iraq to be placed in secret ("black") CIA and military prisons abroad, in Poland and Albania, for example, and most notoriously in the Abu Ghraib prison, located in Baghdad. Additional "detainees" were sent to the American base known as Guantánamo, in Cuba. These suspects languished in prison without legal counsel, the right to habeas corpus (that is, to know the charges brought against them), or a trial. The Administration also authorized the use of torture, such as waterboarding, against some of the prisoners, staining the reputation of the United States abroad. Fear generated by the 9/11 attacks had pushed aside the law and traditional moral values of the United States.

"Preemptive" war in Iraq

The decision of the second Bush Administration to engage in war against Iraq in 2003 proved highly controversial. National Security Adviser Rice, and even President Bush, began to speak publicly about the possibility of "mushroom clouds" appearing on American soil as a result of an Iraq nuclear attack. On September 17, 2002, President Bush released a report entitled *The National Security Strategy of the United States of America*, which outlined what became known as the Bush Doctrine. America would no longer wait to be struck by terrorists; leaders had an obligation, the Administration claimed, to eliminate foreign threats, even if (as in the case of Iraq) they may not have presented an immediate danger.

This approach to the use of force abroad is known by political scientists as "preventive war," mislabeled by the Bush Administration as "preemptive war." In political science theory, preemption is a word reserved for the quick use of force against an adversary who is about to attack immediately. Some find the preventive war approach radical because it invites regimes to use military force prematurely based on a guess an adversary may be planning an attack. Others argue that, especially in an age of nuclear weapons, one cannot afford to wait until an enemy strikes; one has to take the initiative – or perhaps lose millions of citizens in a surprise attack by the enemy.

The Bush Doctrine and the notion of preventive warfare set the stage for "Operation Iraqi Freedom," the Second Persian Gulf War. The invasion in 2003 went smoothly at first, but soon bogged down. The war lost its original mantel of legitimacy when no WMD were found. Further, insurgency warfare against U.S. troops, and between Sunni and Shiite Muslims in Iraq, prevented a quick victory. The president's boast of "mission accomplished" soon proved hollow.

The Obama Administration (2009–2017) began to draw down America's fighting forces in Iraq, as President Barack Obama shifted America's attention back toward Afghanistan and the Taliban. The president sent 30,000 additional troops there, even though Afghanistan is widely known as a "graveyard of invaders." British and Soviet armies suffered major defeats there in the twentieth century, and skeptics doubted the United States would have any greater success. When President Donald J. Trump (2017–2021) came into the White House in 2017, he spoke of removing all U.S. troops from Afghanistan. By the end of his only term, though, the United States still had 2,500 soldiers there. In 2021, President Biden ordered a full drawdown on these troops.

Drone warfare

Although begun by George W. Bush, President Obama ordered a dramatic increase in the number of drone sorties against Qaeda and Taliban encampments in Afghanistan and Pakistan. The drones – Unmanned Aerial Vehicles or UAVs, a fleet consisting primarily of Predators and the larger Reapers – carried surveillance cameras as well as Hellfire missiles, a dangerous combination for America's enemies. These aircraft killed enemy combatants on an almost daily basis, without any American pilots having to risk their lives. The number of drone attacks rose steadily from 2011 through 2019, as the United States became the first nation to conduct UAV strikes regularly against suspected terrorists. The drones were highly unpopular among Pakistani citizens, even those who normally admired the United States, because the deadly flights violated their national sovereignty. Moreover, the UAVs accidentally killed civilians (including a wedding party) from time to time, because of targeting errors. "Top intelligence and military officials," wrote former President Jimmy Carter, "as well as [human] rights defenders in targeted areas, affirm that the great escalation in drone attacks has turned aggrieved families toward terrorist organizations, aroused civilian populations against us and permitted repressive governments to cite such actions to justify their own despotic behavior."

In 2010, U.S. intelligence officials believed that Osama bin Laden was living in the city of Abbottabad, near the Pakistani capital of Islamabad. President Obama rejected a plan for a drone attack against the suspected house, in favor of a more precise assault by a small team of Navy Seals. In the daring mission, the Seals succeeded in killing the Qaeda leader on May 1, 2011, and they confiscated his terrorist operational files from the compound. It was Obama's most significant foreign policy success.

The struggle against terrorism promised to be anything but easy. One concern was the vulnerability of America's computer systems against foreign attack, a policy domain known as cybersecurity. This threat was underscored by the discovery in early 2021 of major Russian cyberattacks against U.S. government facilities. To develop defenses against the possibility of an electronic Pearl Harbor, an operation whereby terrorists or adversaries like Russia would shut down America's communications and computer facilities, President Obama established a Cyber Command within the Pentagon, and Joe Biden, who became president in 2021, appointed the nation's first national security adviser for cyber and emerging technology. The United States was not going to passively accept cyberattacks by the Russians, Chinese, North Koreans, Iranians, or anyone else against the American homeland or U.S. troops overseas.

A time of retrenchment

The Trump presidency was a time of turbulence, to say the least. Donald Trump came across as arrogant to America's allies and, oddly, as a good friend to the Russian dictator, Putin. He withdrew the United States from the Paris Accords, the most important environmental reform efforts the world had seen and endorsed by virtually every other nation. The president also engaged in continual verbal jousting with his intelligence agencies, refusing even to read the *President's Daily Brief* that sums up world events for use in decision-making by top Washington officials – vital information gathered by America's spies around the world and its surveillance satellites and aircraft.

Rather than focus on policy, Trump spent much of his time attending political rallies around the country, working up his followers into a lather over an alleged "deep state" bureaucracy in Washington that was not to be trusted. His most controversial theme: the 2020 presidential election had been stolen from him, even though no evidence existed to confirm that charge. The president's attorneys lost every case they brought to court around the country trying to make this argument; and every state confirmed the integrity of the balloting process that gave the presidential victory to Democrat Joe Biden. The Trump years also were a time of the alarming COVID-19 pandemic that killed over 400,000 Americans in 2020 alone, and millions of other people around the world.

Meanwhile, the president had one aide after another sent to prison for corrupt practices; displayed no interest in doing the daily work expected of a chief executive; and, the crowning glory, encouraged a right-wing mob of disgruntled white supremacists and others who supported his false claims of election fraud to attack the U.S. Capitol in the waning days of his time in office, resulting in the death of five individuals (including a police officer defending the Congress), the destruction of property, and a close call for fleeing or hiding lawmakers who were being hunted down by the insurrectionists. Trump's encouragement of this heinous attack against the pillar of U.S. democracy led to his impeachment in the House of Representatives. Trump ended his turbulent tenure by being the first American president to be impeached twice in a House controlled by Democrats (although never convicted in the GOP-led Senate).

During the Trump years, U.S. foreign policy was self-centered, promoting an isolationist, "America First" agenda rather than working with other democracies against common problems, whether stopping the pandemic, standing up to Putin and his cyberwarriors, tackling environmental degradation, or dealing with hunger and poverty around the globe. America's external relations had entered a low point. In sharp contrast, President Biden brought to the White House a spirit of bipartisanship (he had previously served in the Senate for over three decades), and an understanding of the important role that alliances play in international relations. People around the globe continued to look toward the United States for leadership, given the nation's ongoing military and economic might, plus its example as a strong democracy (despite bad stumbles during the Trump years). Yet, Americans were staggering under the strains of a sluggish economy, rising debt, intense partisan wrangling, and, most of all, the devasting COVID-19 pandemic.

While events, coupled with the narcissistic personality of President Trump, had caused the nation to turn inward again during the Trump years, Biden soon made it clear that he would approach American foreign policy from a liberal internationalist point-of-view. "America is back," he proclaimed in his first major foreign policy speech in February of 2021. He halted Trump's efforts to remove U.S. troops from Germany, a NATO country that preferred to have them there as a shield against possible

Russian military adventurism. "We're going to rebuild our alliances," Biden said, and "reengage the world." As examples, he stressed that his Administration would tackle the pandemic more aggressively, along with the challenges of global warming and restoration of human rights in the world in the face of a growing number of autocratic nations. It was a bold reassertion of U.S. global leadership of the kind that had preceded the Trump Administration.

Notes

For key events during this most recent epoch in American foreign policy, see Madeleine Albright, *Madam Secretary: A Memoir* (New York: Miramax Books, 2003); George Bush and Brent Scowcroft, *A World Transformed* (New York: Knopf, 1998); Loch K. Johnson, *The Threat on the Horizon* (New York: Oxford University Press, 2011), the source for the "aerial terrorism" quote: 123; Fred Kaplan, *The Insurgents: David Petraeus and the Plot to Change the American Way of War* (New York: Simon & Schuster, 2013); and Paul R. Pillar, *Intelligence and U.S. Foreign Policy: Iraq, 9/11, and Misguided Reform* (New York: Columbia University Press, 2011). The Woolsey quote is from his testimony, *Hearings*, Select Committee on Intelligence, U.S. Senate, 103d Cong., 2d Sess. (March 6, 1993); the Kennan quote, from "Breakup of the Soviet Union," *Great Decisions*, Foreign Policy Association (1992): 82; and the President Carter quote, from his "A Cruel and Unusual Record," *The New York Times* (June 25, 2012): A17.

PART III

The making of foreign policy

6 The constitutional framework

America's founders were imbued with an anti-power perspective on governance. By distributing power across institutions, they hoped to limit its potential for abuse. With responsibilities and prerogatives spread over the executive, legislative, and judicial branches of government, the constitutional framers reasoned that no branch would grow so mighty as to dwarf the others or dictate to the American people. "The greatest insight of our Founding Fathers," concluded Senator Frank Church, Chair of the Senate Foreign Relations Committee in the 1980s, "was their recognition of the dangers of unlimited power exercised by a single man or institution. Their greatest achievement was the safeguards against absolute power which they wrote into our Constitution." Yet how could one coordinate and integrate these dispersed units of government, each with formidable powers? Would separate entities really share power and work together for the good of the nation? The answers remained in doubt, particularly since the very Constitution that gave the three branches their authority seemed to present, with all of its silences and ambiguities, "an invitation to struggle," in Professor Edward S. Corwin's memorable phrase.

Those who drafted the Constitution were prudent to concern themselves with the dangers of concentrated power. Few observers of history would deny the truth of Lord Acton's famous aphorism: "Power corrupts, and absolute power corrupts absolutely." Yet in their headlong escape from tyranny, had the founders embraced another serious threat to democracy: an institutional paralysis resulting from a government excessively fragmented? If at one end of a power continuum stood the dangers of absolute power, at the other end stood anarchy. Can collaborative government work, especially when dealing with the often tangled and perilous challenges of international affairs?

Foreign policy and the Constitution

While the phrases "foreign policy" or "foreign affairs" appear nowhere in the Constitution, America's founding document did spell out the basic authorities of the president and the Congress in carrying forth the nation's responsibilities in international relations. The president's powers are addressed in Article II, Section 2. They are relatively meager: "The Executive Power shall be vested in a President," who "shall take Care that the Laws be faithfully executed." The president had the authority to make treaties, but these international agreements had to be based on the "Advice and Consent of the Senate" and approved by two-thirds of the senators. Further, the president could appoint U.S. ambassadors, as well as "receive Ambassadors and other public Ministers ..." from other countries, but this remains a rather limited duty except when controversy brews over whether a new nation should be officially recognized by the United States. More empowering was the president's designation as "Commander-in-Chief of the Army and Navy of the United States." It was up to the Congress, however, "To provide for the common Defense ... To declare War ... To Raise and support Armies ... To provide and maintain a Navy."

The Constitution spells out the powers of the legislative branch chiefly in Article I. Preeminent among them is the power of the purse: "No money shall be drawn from the Treasury, but in Consequence of Appropriations made by Law." The president is unable to spend one thin dime without a congressional authorization and appropriation. If lawmakers wish to curb a presidential action, they can withhold funding. The Congress was also expected to "To regulate commerce with foreign nations," as well as "make all Laws which shall be necessary and proper." Moreover, lawmakers have the authority to impeach and convict a president.

Much has changed in the world in the 234 years since the writing of the Constitution in Philadelphia. The American government now has a large bureaucracy; Congress has grown into a complicated warren of committees and subcommittees; political parties have become more important. The United States has grown large, and scores of new nations have come into existence, weapons of mass destruction have been invented, and news now travels at lightning speed, as do missiles and stealth bombers. Throughout these changes, though, one principle has remained constant:

in a constitutional government, important decisions are supposed to rest on the consent of both the legislature and the president, each democratically elected. This principle has been sorely tested, though, on the contentious issues of war- and treaty-making.

The war power

Defensive versus offensive warfare

A misinterpretation of Article II, Section 2 of the Constitution sometimes leads to the unwarranted conclusion that the president enjoys preeminent authority over the war power. Properly understood, this section gives to the president the right and obligation as commander in chief to *repel* sudden attacks against the United States, when a delay to consult with Congress would be foolhardy, even suicidal. The president, however, was not allowed to *initiate* hostilities. Nevertheless, an erosion of legislative control over the war power occurred, slowly at first and then in the twentieth century with increasing speed. The twin catastrophes of the Great Depression and the Second World War were both powerful catalysts for a concentration of power in the White House.

This suited the temperament of President Franklin D. Roosevelt. In the worthy battle against the Axis powers, not only was he willing to usurp the treaty power through his destroyers-for-bases deal with Britain (carried out as an executive agreement), but he also sought a more exclusive control over the war power than any other president since Lincoln. For example, in 1941 Roosevelt assigned U.S. warships to accompany, all the way to Iceland, American convoys loaded with supplies for the British. By himself, the president had done nothing less than draw the United States into undeclared naval warfare in the Atlantic Ocean. By eliding the constitutional authorities of Congress, Roosevelt had established a dubious precedent for war-making that his successors could rely on for more questionable purposes.

Inherent presidential authority

Each of the presidents since the Second World War from Harry S. Truman to Donald Trump has tended to view the war power from the vantage point of Franklin Roosevelt. For each, the belief has endured that only Congress has the authority to declare war formally; however, many executive officials, seemed to think that – short of a formal declaration of war – the president as commander-in-chief enjoys the right to use the military option as the White House sees fit, as though America's soldiers and sailors were so many chess pieces and the president the grandmaster. In 1950, for instance, President Truman made the decision to commit American troops to the war in Korea – a "police action," in the Administration's phrase – without congressional authorization. For the first time, the White House had evoked a doctrine that claimed an inherent constitutional right of presidential dominance over the decision to make war.

In 1951, leading conservative Senator Robert Taft of Ohio (R-Ohio) grumbled that "the President simply usurped authority, in violation of the laws and the Constitution, when he sent troops to Korea to carry out the resolution of the United Nations in an undeclared war." In 2011, President Obama would invoke his rights as president to provide support for a NATO coalition fighting against the dictator of Libya, so long as the president did not use U.S. ground troops – a new wrinkle in the "inherent authority" argument.

War by blank check

President Dwight D. Eisenhower proved to be shrewder than either FDR or Truman about executive claims to broad, inherent war powers. He requested from lawmakers permission to use military force by way of a congressional resolution, requiring a majority vote in both legislative chambers in support of a policy initiative. Eisenhower asked on several occasions for authority from Congress to use the armed forces in various parts of the world and its members readily complied. In fact, lawmakers provided broad grants of authority to employ force "as [the president] determines necessary."

Caught up in the exigencies of the moment, the legislative branch had lost sight of its own constitutional standing. Lawmakers left the unfortunate impression that Congress had accepted the concept of full presidential discretionary authority over the use of military force, and that the role of lawmakers was merely to express a sense of national unity as the president strove to protect America's "vital interests" abroad. In a subsequent review of these presidential initiatives, the Senate Foreign Relations Committee (SFRC) expressed concern that "an authorization so general and imprecise amounts to an unconstitutional alienation of its war power on the part of the Congress."

The resolutions deemed so repugnant to the SFRC had been passed by Congress in 1955 at the request of President Eisenhower to defend Formosa (Taiwan) and the Pescadores (islands located between Formosa and mainland China), as well as nations in the Middle East in 1957. The most fateful of the foreign policy resolutions passed by Congress, however, was the Gulf of Tonkin Resolution, approved in August of 1964, at the request of President Lyndon Johnson. Reacting to intelligence reports provided by the executive branch claiming that U.S. naval vessels off the coast of Vietnam had come under enemy fire, lawmakers hastily declared in this resolution that "the Congress approves and supports the determination of the President, as Commander in Chief, to take all necessary measures to repel any armed attack against the forces of the United States and to prevent further aggression." The measure passed 533-to-2.

The erosion of legislative control over the war power had reached an extreme; Congress seemed to acknowledge practically unlimited control to the White House over the use of military force. After the vote, Undersecretary of State Nicholas Katzenbach pointed to the Tonkin Resolution as the "functional equivalent" of a declaration of war by Congress. Yet, according to Senator Church, "Congress neither expected nor even considered at the time of the debate on the resolution that the President would later commit more than half a million American soldiers to a full-scale war in Vietnam." Moreover, the intelligence reports of 1964 proved to have been incorrect.

The treaty power

The struggle between the branches over the control of foreign policy extended into the domain of diplomacy as well. By virtue of the Constitution, the Congress and the executive branch share the authority to establish America's diplomatic commitments abroad. The only explicit reference to international agreement-making in the document is the treaty provision of Article II, Section 2. This passage states that the president "shall have power, by and with the advice of the Senate to make treaties, provided two-thirds of the Senators present concur." These words convey the idea of a partnership between the legislative and executive branches. The executive branch obviously plays a central role in the treaty procedure, including the final right of ratification (a word often wrongly attributed in the media to the Senate's approval vote); however, the wording of Article II, Section 2 also undeniably provides the Senate a central role as well. The practice of the modern executive branch has drifted far away from the treaty-making principles of the nation's founders.

The executive branch has often simply bypassed the Constitution's treaty procedure. During the early stages of the Cold War, for instance, a scant 6 percent of America's international agreements were approved through the formal treaty process. In its place have arisen two additional forms of international agreement-making. First, some pacts with other nations have been based on loosely worded statutes that grant permission to the executive branch to move ahead on an agreement. This approach is known as a "statutory agreement" and at least has the merit of legislative involvement. Second are international transactions carried out by the executive branch alone, absent any meaningful consultation with the Congress and sometimes hidden altogether from lawmakers. They are known as "executive agreements." Reliance by the executive branch on statutory and executive agreements has remained consist in recent years, even though every now and then presidents have negotiated treaties of substantial importance, such as the Panama Canal Treaties of 1978.

The war in Vietnam provided a rude awakening for the legislative branch. The unpopular uses of presidential power in Indochina, and the even more blatant manifestation of presidential arrogance in the Watergate scandal, would turn the attention of lawmakers back to forgotten questions of constitutional authority – especially regarding the treaty and the war powers. (The measures adopted by Congress to restore its eroded authority are examined in later chapters.) Institutional strife will continue to be a hallmark of American government. What else would one expect from a system willfully fractured by the nation's founders to thwart the concentration – and, therefore, potential abuse – of power? As the leading drafter of the Constitution, James Madison argued in *Federalist Papers No. 51* that "the great security against a gradual concentration of the several powers in the same department consists in giving to those who administer each department the necessary constitutional means and personal motives to resist encroachments of the others ... Ambition must be made to counteract ambition."

The founders embraced this prescription and the result, doubtless, is a government less prone to tyranny. Critics argue, though, that the costs may be too high, that the United States is unable to compete effectively in the global arena against autocracies, where rulers can make fast decisions.

According to this anti-Madisonian argument, the world is too small, events move too quickly, secrecy is too important, weapons have become too dangerous for the luxury of traditional constitutional checks and balances, for Congress to do anything more than support executive decisions on foreign affairs. This perspective is evaluated in the next chapters, where America's institutional arrangements for the conduct of foreign policy are examined more closely.

Notes

Much valuable research has been published on the tensions between the executive and legislative branches in the conduct of foreign affairs. See, for example, Raoul Berger, "The Presidential Monopoly of Foreign Relations," *Michigan Law Review* 71 (1972): 24–42; Edward S. Corwin, *The President: Office and Powers* (New York: New York University Press, 1957); Louis Fisher, *Defending Congress and the Constitution* (Lawrence: University Press of Kansas, 2011); and Louis Henkin, *Foreign Affairs and the United States Constitution* (Oxford: Clarendon, 1996). The SFRC quote is from Foreign Relations Committee, "National Commitments," *Report No. 91-129*, U.S. Senate (April 16, 1969), Washington, D.C.: 20;

and the Frank Church quote is from Loch K. Johnson, "Operational Codes and the Prediction of Leadership Behavior," in Margaret G. Herman, ed., *A Psychological Examination of Political Man* (New York: Free Press, 1977): 89.

7   Institutional conflict and cooperation

In the philosophy underlying the U.S. Constitution, efficiency was not the prime value. If it had been, the authors of the document would have given the presidency greater power – or even created an absolute monarchy. On the contrary, as constitutional specialist Laurence H. Tribe has noted, "the framers were unwilling to give the President anything resembling royal prerogative." Through their rejection of sweeping executive powers, they hoped to shield the new Republic – and posterity – from the dangers of autocratic rule. By rejecting royal prerogative, however, the founders created a government that often displays signs of sluggishness, parochialism, and disarray. They had crafted precisely what Winston S. Churchill once said a democracy would always be: the worst possible form of government – except for all the others that have been tried from time to time.

President versus lawmakers

A central issue of American foreign policy is the degree to which it ought to be an executive branch responsibility or, as in domestic policy, the United States should have a wide range of participants involved – and certainly the representatives of the American people in Congress. One can imagine a presidential model of foreign policy in which global decisions would be left exclusively to the White House and senior bureaucrats; or a legislative model, in which key decisions would be left solely to lawmakers.

The presidential model enjoys widespread support in some quarters for the reason of efficiency. Moreover, a strong sense exists in this school of thought that, to be taken seriously in world affairs, the United States must speak with one voice – the president's. Some lawmakers have adopted this view, happily passing along responsibility to the White House for tangled problems overseas that might spell trouble in the next election. Many other members of Congress, though, have opposed foreign policy by executive fiat. Even before Vietnam and Watergate raised serious doubts about an uncritical reliance on presidential power, a pro-Congress viewpoint was well established, especially on the conservative side of the American political spectrum. Isolationists, for example, looked upon the presidency as the agent of interventionism abroad, leading to an unacceptable drain on American resources.

Another school of thought, though, points out that lawmakers are closer to the grass roots and, as a result, they have a better understanding of what citizens from Los Angeles, California, to Portland, Maine, expect in their nation's foreign policy. According to this perspective, members of Congress are like raw nerve endings reaching into each of the 50 states and the 435 congressional districts across the land, gauging the likely public response to vital issues of foreign policy. While the president cannot possibly visit each congressional district, lawmakers visit their constituencies usually every week – some every day, if their districts are close to Washington, D.C. This makes Congress a unique, continuous forum of timely public opinion.

A foreign policy compact

In between the presidential and legislative models of foreign policy-making lies another approach, which might be called the "model of power sharing." Here the emphasis is on cooperation between co-equal legislative and executive branches of government: an engine with all its cylinders firing. President George H. W. Bush demonstrated the value of a common effort between the branches. In 1989, when Chinese troops attacked pro-reform students in Beijing, Bush immediately called key lawmakers to the White House and worked out with them a strategy of public criticism and economic sanctions as a punishment for Beijing's slaying of peaceful demonstrators.

President Jimmy Carter's Undersecretary of State, Warren M. Christopher (later, Secretary of State in the Clinton Administration), framed the argument for interbranch cooperation in terms of an executive-legislative compact. "As a fundamental precept," he wrote, "the compact would call for restraint on the part of the Congress – for Congress to recognize and accept the responsibility of the Executive to conduct and manage foreign policy on a daily basis." In return, the executive branch needed to provide Congress with "full information and consultation." He went on: "Broad policy should be jointly designed" and only in rare extreme circumstances should Congress attempt "to dictate or overturn Executive decisions and actions."

As one looks at the institutional side of foreign policy, something resembling each of these models can be observed at different times. Sometimes the president is able to gather together enough fragments of power to achieve ascendancy over a decision, especially in times of perceived emergency to the nation's security; sometimes the Congress shapes foreign policy, as when it led the creation of NATO in 1949; and sometimes the two branches work together toward a policy decision, as Joe Biden intends with climate reform. No single model is sufficient to explain America's relations with other countries, although the sharing model best reflects the intention of the Constitution.

The presidency

Despite the fabled red telephone on the president's desk that could initiate a third world war, and despite the guaranteed access a president has to the people of the United States through television and radio, studies reveal that nothing so defines the nation's highest office as its limitations. One of the primary limitations on the president is the international setting. Regardless of how skilled a chief executive may be, the events a president faces can be unmanageable. Reflecting on the foreign policy setbacks of the Carter Administration, the president's National Security Adviser, Zbigniew Brzezinski, expressed dismay at the inability of Washington to control events abroad. Particularly vexing had been the fate of American hostages held in Tehran by Iranian insurgents from November of 1979 until the end of the Carter Administration, 14 months later. "History is much more the product of chaos than of conspiracy," concluded Brzezinski. "The external world's vision of internal decision-making in the Government assumes too much cohesion and expects too much systematic planning. The fact of the matter is that, increasingly, policy makers are overwhelmed by events and information."

Information and time

Brzezinski's stress on the problem of information is warranted. Government leaders find that they either have too much or too little information about world affairs. On the one hand, they can be inundated by data. The early warning predicting a Japanese attack on Pearl Harbor in 1941 provides one illustration. America's intelligence agencies had intercepted coded Japanese messages about the impending attack, but this information was lost in the "noise" of conflicting reports from a variety of other intelligence sources. The key messages floundered in the lower realms of the bureaucracy and President Roosevelt never received the warning. And, on the other hand, insufficient information is even more common. Nations are often caught unprepared, because of a lack of reporting on the activities of their enemies. In the months leading up to the 9/11 attacks the United States knew little about Al Qaeda and its plans for aerial terrorism against the American homeland. Improvements in intelligence gathering have reduced this danger; but no administration has a crystal ball and unexpected events will continue to occur.

Time is another limitation faced by all decision-makers. The Cuban Missile Crisis provides a vivid example. "If we had had to act in the first twenty-four hours," reflected President Kennedy, "I don't think ... we would have chosen as prudently as we finally did." The president would have been forced to take military action, rather than consider other options like the quarantine he finally chose to impose against Russian missile-bearing ships.

Resources

Government programs cost money. Yet a president inevitably faces limits on how much funding is available, or the extent to which taxes can be raised without wreaking havoc on the economy or stirring a taxpayer rebellion. Lyndon Johnson's attempt to rebuild the cities of America and fight a war in Vietnam simultaneously proved too costly, fueling inflation and leading to the unpopularity that drove him from office. Money is only one governmental resource. Others include the number of soldiers available to fight a war; the quantity and quality of weapons in a nation's arsenal; the will or determination of a populace to pursue a difficult course overseas; the credibility of a president; a nation's industrial output; and a nation's supply of brilliant generals and civilian advisers.

Formal powers

Even the formal powers of the presidency are less potent than frequently believed. Expressing his own sense of exasperation about foreign policy, President Johnson once exclaimed: "Power? The only power I've got is nuclear – and I can't use that." The powers of the presidency are few in number and largely outmatched on most occasions by the limitations on the office, even when coupled with the advantage of ready access to the media enjoyed by the chief executive. A look at the executive bureaucracy – both a check on presidential power and sometimes a tool for its excesses – corroborates this observation.

The foreign policy bureaucracy

The Department of State has a seemingly endless number of corridors in its many-storied complex; and the Department of Defense, the giant of them all, is a honeycomb of passageways that could stymie the most accomplished orienteer. To improve the integration of the departments and agencies dealing with foreign policy, the Congress enacted the National Security Act of 1947, which established a National Security Council.

The NSC is the most important organization in the federal bureaucracy when it comes to foreign affairs. It consists of three primary groups: the principals (the president, the vice president, the Secretary of State, and the Secretary of Defense); the advisers (the Director of National Intelligence and the Chair of the Joint Chiefs of Staff, with others invited to attend NSC meetings from time to time); and the professional staff of experts. The bridge that connects all three groups is the National Security Adviser. As Colin Powell, who served as Adviser under President Reagan, once put it: "I was to perform as judge, traffic cop, truant officer, arbitrator, fireman, chaplain, psychiatrist, and occasional hit man." Above all, the position has evolved into the role of an honest broker to mediate disputes among the cabinet departments, and especially to mollify as much as possible the institutional tensions between the State and Defense Departments, serving as a bridge between the two. Brent Scowcroft, considered by many to be the quintessential honest broker when he served (twice) as Adviser, observed: "... if you are not the honest broker, you don't have the confidence of the other members of the NSC. If you don't have their confidence, then the system doesn't work, because they will go around you to get to the president and then you fracture the system."

Departments of State and Defense

The two oldest departments in the government are State and Defense (the latter known as the Department of War until 1947). They remain the most influential of the foreign policy bureaucracies. The secretary of state is the first-ranking cabinet member and is widely considered the chief foreign policy adviser to the president. That role is sometimes wrestled away from the secretary by activist national security advisers, though, who since the 1960s have had the advantage of nearness to the president; they occupy an office just down the hallway from the Oval Office in the West Wing of the White House. Whether the secretary is able to serve as the president's top foreign policy person depends on the personal chemistry between the two, as well as how talented and aggressive the secretary is.

At the heart of the State Department is the Foreign Service, which is responsible for the day-to-day conduct of America's relations with other countries. The men and women of the Foreign Service, who serve in Washington and in U.S. embassies overseas, prepare reports that help shape foreign policy decisions. The top American official in a U.S. embassy is the ambassador, who in about two-thirds of the cases since 1950 has been a career State Department officer; the other one-third are political appointees. Inside the State Department in Washington reside the country desk officers, the men and women who keep daily watch over all the major countries around the globe, reading the secret and non-secret cables and other documents that stream into the State Department from U.S. embassies, and who keep the secretary of state well informed.

The most imposing of all the organizations involved in American foreign policy is the Department of Defense (DoD). Within its institutional framework are large standing military forces: more than three million employees, along with 750 military bases in 130 countries. Several of the bases are new and located in the Middle East and Southwest Asia, in places like Bahrain, Kyrgyzstan, United Arab Emirates, Qatar, Iraq and Afghanistan. The DoD secretary is often viewed as an 800 lb gorilla in the cabinet because of the size of annual defense budgets. Over US$700 billion a year in recent times, the annual Defense Department budget dwarfs the spending of the State Department, which garners some US$50 billion a year.

The magnitude and number of foreign programs and operations conducted by the Departments of State and Defense alone would be enough to keep a conscientious president burning the midnight oil. Yet these behemoths represent only a fraction of the foreign policy leadership challenge. Almost every major agency in the government has an international component involved in negotiations of one kind or another with other nations, frequently with little or no guidance or control from the White House or the State Department. Madison was right: the president needs help from the Congress in supervising the conduct of American foreign policy, especially as the number and scope of bureaucratic agencies has proliferated.

The Congress

Members of the Senate and the House often insist on being counted in the making of America's foreign policy. Furthermore, they have enacted statutes that mandate executive-branch reports to various committees and subcommittees on a range of policy proposals. Congress is no longer willing to be kept in the dark and these reporting requirements are designed to shed light on the intentions of the White House and the bureaucracy. In an attitude of defiance, Representative Carl Vinson (D-Georgia), chairman of the House Armed Services Committee, informed the Secretary of Defense in 1949 that "Congress won't be bypassed, and we will be conversant with what goes on." A similar spirit of independence pervaded many members of the legislative branch in the wake of Vietnam, Watergate, and a CIA domestic spy scandal in the mid-1970s. While this congressional ardor for a co-partnership in foreign policy has cooled somewhat in recent years, as lawmakers run away from the heavy responsibilities of warfare in the Middle East and Southwest

Asia, many members of Congress continue to insist on respect from the executive branch for the constitutional prerogatives of the legislative branch.

The courts

The Supreme Court had little to say about foreign policy for the first 150 years of America's existence. In recent decades, though, U.S. courts have entered into foreign policy disputes, and they usually back the White House. Now and then, though, judges have trimmed back the president's authority. For example, the so-called Pentagon Papers case (*New York Times Co.* v. *United States*, heard by the Supreme Court in 1971) came out against President Nixon's request to prevent the *Times* and other papers from publishing the Pentagon's classified, in-house history of the Vietnamese war. By a 5-to-4 vote, the Court concluded that nothing within these research papers, if published, would lead to "irreparable harm" to the United States. The Congress and the American people were allowed to read the DoD study about America's conduct of the war in Vietnam – a signal from the Court that the executive branch could not cover up questionable decisions simply by classifying documents as "top secret" and hiding them from the public.

The complexities of leadership

Foreign policy leadership in the United States relies primarily on bargaining between the Congress and the White House, and only rarely on simple command from a president. "Presidential power is the power to persuade," observed political scientist Richard E. Neustadt. Researchers have found that when acting as commander-in-chief the president is most powerful, especially when the nation is threatened from abroad. Next, in the role of chief diplomat, the president's powers remain considerable, for the Constitution and custom give the president clear prerogatives in this area. Presidential authority becomes progressively weaker, however, with the president's roles as chief executive over the bureaucracy, as legislative leader, and, the least powerful of all, as public opinion and party leader. These roles rely less on constitutional or statutory authority than on the president's abilities to persuade. In matters of power in Washington, D.C., circumstances can be important, too. "If Lincoln had lived in a time of peace," Theodore Roosevelt once observed, "no one would have known his name."

Notes

On the subject of institutional conflict and cooperation in U.S. foreign policy, see Cecil V. Crabb and Pat M. Holt, *Invitation to Struggle: Congress, the President, and Foreign Policy,* (Washington, D.C.: CQ Press, 1984); Thomas M. Franck and Edward Weisband, *Foreign Policy by Congress* (New York: Oxford University Press, 1979); Jack Goldsmith, *Power and Constraint: The Accountable President After 9/11* (New York: Norton, 2012); Theodore C. Sorensen, *Decision-Making in the White House* (New York: Columbia University Press, 1963); Raymond Tatalovich and Byron W. Daynes, *Presidential Power in the United States* (Belmont, CA: Brooks/ Cole, 1984); and Stephen R. Weissman, *A Culture of Deference: Congress's Failure of Leadership in Foreign Policy* (New York: HarperCollins, 1994). On the National Security Council, see Karl F. Inderfurth and Loch K. Johnson, eds., *Fateful Decisions: Inside the National Security Council* (New York: Oxford University Press, 2004). For the quotes in this chapter, see: Tribe, cited in *The New York Times* (May 17, 1987): A1; Warren Christopher, "Ceasefire between the Branches: A Compact in Foreign Affairs," *Foreign Affairs* 60 (Summer 1982): 999; Brzezinski, quoted in *The New York Times* (January 18, 1981): A3; Colin Powell, with Joseph E. Perisco, *My American Journey* (New York: Random House, 1995): 352; Scowcroft, in Inderfurth and Johnson, *Fateful Decisions*: 138; Vinson, in Vance Packard, "Uncle Carl, Watchdog of Defense," *American Magazine* 149 (April 1950): 123; Richard E. Neustadt, *Presidential Power* (New York: Wiley, 1980): 4; and Edmund Morris, *Colonel Roosevelt* (New York: Random House, 2010).

8   The human dimension

Individuals can make a difference in the drama of American foreign policy. Personalities matter. "Political science without biography," observed political scientist Harold Lasswell, "is a form of taxidermy." A pioneer in the analysis of personality and politics, he understood that although a knowledge of political institutions was important to the study of public policy, so was the behavior of individuals, whether in public opinion polls, in the voting booth, as members of pressure groups, or in high office.

Public opinion

Elections seldom turn on issues of foreign policy, unless the nation is at war. Voters are usually most concerned about the state of the domestic economy: basic pocketbook issues, such as the level of unemployment or inflation, or their access to good health care. While the ballot box remains the most crucial means of public expression in a democracy, few successful politicians have been prepared simply to ignore voters until election time; they try to gauge opinion in between their campaigns for re-election.

Most of the time, the American people remain in a state of ignorance about the details of international affairs. Important U.S.-Canadian trade negotiations, for example, pass virtually unnoticed by most citizens. Only 35 percent of American citizens possess a passport (compared to 80 percent in the United Kingdom); and in recent presidential elections, only 4 percent of the American public indicated in national surveys that foreign policy was important in their balloting. Even when the public is aroused, as when the Nixon Administration expanded the Vietnamese war into Cambodia in 1970, opinion can be so diverse and conflicting that no clear signal emerges from the public. As a result, policymakers are usually free to rely on their own personal judgments.

While most voters have little specific information about foreign affairs, they are able to express meaningful views on the general direction the United States is taking overseas. In 1968, for example, Americans made plain enough its dislike for President Johnson's Vietnam War policies. In the United States, two conditions are most likely to stir an awakening of public opinion: first, prolonged military conflict with no victory in sight and, second, bleak economic news – inflation, rising interest rates, a dramatic plunge in the stock market, high unemployment, an unfavorable Consumer Price Index, and, above all, a depression or recession. The lives of U.S. soldiers overseas and the family checkbook – peace and prosperity. These matters count the most in the public eye.

The rally-round-the-flag phenomenon

A question of particular interest to students of international affairs is how the public responds, as indicated by opinion polls, to the most extreme use of foreign policy power: military force. The "rally-round-the-flag" hypothesis provides one answer. This concept states that a perceived threat to the United States will result in a display by the American public of strong patriotic support for the president, sending the standing of the chief executive sharply upward in opinion ratings on job performance. This rallying response seems to occur, though, only during certain kinds of events. For instance, they must involve a rapid military intervention by the United States abroad, say in Korea in 1950 and Afghanistan in 2001, or significant military developments in an ongoing war, such as President Johnson's response to the Gulf of Tonkin incident in 1964. Examples of the rally response are abundant. Among the most conspicuous was a confrontation in Cambodia in 1975. Use of the Marines in a rescue attempt of U.S. merchant marines captured by the Cambodians led to an 11-point surge in President Ford's approval rating in the polls, even though the rescue failed. The Grenada invasion in 1983 boosted President Reagan's standing in the polls by four percentage points, however insignificant this island was to U.S. security.

Researchers who have examined the rally phenomenon more closely discovered a missing ingredient in the argument. Important is the availability of information to the public that could call into question the merits of a presidential decision. When the second Bush Administration claimed that Iraq had hidden WMD that could be used against the United States, for instance, the American people had no reliable information to the contrary; therefore, they rallied behind the president. In these situations, even national leaders who might be critical of an Administration's claims – say, congressional leaders in the opposition party – are in a weak position to offer a persuasive critique; therefore, they are inclined to be supportive. Or at least they remain quiescent; and when opinion leaders remain silent the general public has no alternative source of information or guidance from respected officials as to why they should question a presidential decision. Safe from criticism, for the time being at any rate, the White House decision gains public support, thanks to a president's monopoly over information about unfolding events. As researchers Brody and Shapiro point out, "... a lack of critical opinion leadership can outweigh even relatively unambiguous evidence of policy failure and hence pave the way for positive evaluations of presidential performance."

Congress and public opinion

What can be said about the relationship between lawmakers and public opinion? Political theorists often discuss this subject in terms of a classic dichotomy: a representative may be a "trustee" making decisions strictly on the basis of his or her own judgment; or he or she may behave as an "instructed delegate" who attempts to mirror the opinion of constituents back home. The British conservative Edmund Burke dismissed the instructed-delegate model of representation with a famous rebuke: "Your representative owes you, not his industry only, but his judgement; and he betrays, instead of serving you, if he sacrifices it to your opinion." Despite the acclaim for this independent stance that rises above the whims of public opinion, often referred to as the "Burkean model" of representation, most elected officials in the United States attempt to read the tea leaves of public opinion as best they can.

Public opinion polls usually rank last as a barometer of constituency opinion. Part of the problem is their broad focus. With some exceptions, they are national or regional in scope; therefore, members of Congress must make a considerable extrapolation to assume the opinions on foreign affairs expressed in these polls are reflective of views held by citizens in their smaller constituencies. Researchers consistently confirm that most members of Congress believe their mail is the single best indicator of constituent attitudes. The use of e-mails, text-messaging, tweeting, and other social media has amplified the significance of more traditional "letter" communications from back home. For foreign policy, some political scientists have also suggested a modern twist to the Burkean model of representation: a "model of presidential deference." According to this argument, in the case of foreign policy lawmakers are freed from constituent pressures because on such matters the public is ill-informed and inattentive; yet, rather than exercise their own judgment in a Burkean fashion, lawmakers are inclined to defer to presidential leadership, because of all the information the White House has access to – from the CIA, State and Defense, and myriad other bureaucracies staffed by experts.

As evidence for the rally-round-the-flag hypothesis indicates, under some circumstances the model of presidential deference is preeminent. Members of Congress, though, have grown less trustful of White House leadership since the failed war in Vietnam, along with the Watergate scandal, domestic spy scandals, the Iran-*contra* intelligence scandal, controversial wars in Iraq and Afghanistan, and misgivings about White House leadership under the distracted Donald Trump. This decline in presidential deference is more in line with the philosophy of the Constitution. A pooling of policy knowledge and responsibility by both the executive and legislative branches of government is the genius of governance envisioned by America's founders. Yet other lawmakers have recently turned to an additional approach to foreign policy decision-making decisions – the "party loyalty model," whereby members of Congress simply vote along party lines. Until recently, such voting had been rare in the U.S. Congress; but, starting in the early 1990s, partisanship became heated on Capitol Hill and members have increasingly voted along strict party lines.

On most occasions, the foreign policy views of the general public are less likely to be taken into account, day by day, than those of citizens who have organized themselves into interest groups for the purpose of promoting their policy objectives.

Interest groups

An astonishing array of interest (or "pressure") groups in the United States attempts to influence foreign policy. They enjoy the constitutional authority to advocate their views, based on the Constitution's First Amendment right to "peaceably to assemble, and to petition the Government for a redress of grievances." Every conceivable interest seems to be represented in the nation's Capital, including such groups as Amnesty International, Women's International League for Peace and Freedom, Council for a Livable World, and the Committee for a Sane Nuclear Policy. In addition, there are oil companies, textile industries, veterans, peace movements, trade associations, shipping interests, airline interests, farmers, human rights activists, animal rights advocates – the list goes on.

The range of goals, and methods of lobbying, are as diverse as the groups themselves. Not only do legitimate lobbyists and the people they represent have a right to be heard, but many of them bring to the government useful information and ideas that can elevate the quality of policy deliberations. Yet marked inequities exist. Well-heeled corporations – with their well-connected lobbyists and sizable treasure chest of campaign funds – enjoy far greater success in bringing their case to top officials in Washington than small groups operating on a shoestring.

Some of the lobbyists who descend on Washington with foreign policy demands represent the interests of other nations. The American Jewish community, for example, has been successful in pressuring the U.S. government for enormous sums of foreign aid earmarked for Israel. Sizable caches of weapons are also sold at special rates to the Israelis – one of the grievances enumerated by Al Qaeda for its attacks against the United States in 2001. The community's chief lobbying arm is the American Israel Public Affairs Committee (AIPAC), which works with scores of allied organizations around the country under the umbrella of the Council of Presidents of Major American Jewish Organizations. This careful nurturing of the powerful in Washington by AIPAC and its allies pays off. The American aid package to Israel each year is worth over US$3 billion, which was the largest for any country until Afghanistan took precedence in recent years.

Significant as lobbying interests, too, have been various global corporations and international organizations operating outside the framework of national governments. In the 1970s, the U.S. corporation International Telephone and Telegraph (ITT) demonstrated its clout at the White House by applying strong pressure on the Nixon Administration to intervene on its behalf in Chile. The corporation sought to overthrow the Chilean leader, Salvador Allende, whom they feared might expropriate its holdings in that nation. The Administration succeeded in this coup.

The military-industrial-intelligence complex is another set of influential lobbying organizations. The manufacturers of expensive weaponry and spy satellites, along with the network of consultants, think tanks, and laboratories that surround them, have a clear economic stake in maintaining a high budget for national defense. So do politicians, labor unions, and a host of other beneficiaries in many states. A recent Saudi arms deal lost to Britain carried with it some 50,000 new jobs for the weapons-manufacturing sector. Weapons like the laser-beam shield against foreign missilry, advocated by the Reagan Administration (the Strategic Defense Initiative, or "Star Wars"), can mean huge sums of federal funding for a state's economy. Some researchers believe, however, that these components of the military-industrial-intelligence complex are really of secondary importance for understanding America's embrace of large U.S. defense budgets. The more fundamental driving force during the Cold War was, in their view, the ongoing fear and distrust toward the Soviet Union held by the American public and, at the time, fueled by the rhetoric of the Reagan Administration.

Often more important to foreign policy than broad public opinion or specific group opinion, though, are the beliefs of individual decision-makers. This micro level of foreign policy analysis focuses on the behavior of individuals in high office.

The individual

Lasswell was sensitive to the influence that early, private events in the life of a political leader could exert on his or her later public decisions. He defined "political man" (*homo politicus*) as a power-seeker, driven primarily by a desire to overcome feelings of inferiority engendered by unpleasant experiences in early life. "Power," Lasswell wrote, "is expected to overcome low estimates of the self." With obvious Freudian antecedents, Lasswell attempted to link the low self-esteem of the youth to power-seeking in the adult.

Employing the Lasswellian hypothesis, studies have explored the life of Woodrow Wilson (among other leaders), tracing back his intransigence toward senators over the League of Nations proposal to the president's early childhood relationship with his father, a prominent clergyman in Virginia. In odd emotional outbursts, Wilson refused to compromise with the Senate and especially with Henry Cabot Lodge, the chairman of the Foreign Relations Committee. Searching through his early record, scholars find evidence of low self-esteem in the young Wilson. Cowed by a domineering father, Wilson seemed stymied in his maturation, fearful that he might be unable to reach the lofty expectations his father had set for him. According to this research, Wilson later sought political power as a means for proving his worthiness to himself and to his father. When confronted by opponents like Lodge, Wilson lashed out irrationally at what he perceived to a be a manifestation of attempts to dominate him again, just as his father had done.

Ego defense versus statecraft

This Freudian approach lacks appeal to many students of political behavior. A major objection is the theory's unscientific nature, in the sense of failing to provide an opportunity for testing and disproving ("falsifying") the central hypothesis, as one can (for instance) Einstein's equations on relativity. The Freudian explanation requires a leap of faith. One can only evaluate whether this kind of theory appears to fit the available facts and defeats alternative explanations – a less satisfying test than the rigors of modern scientific empiricism demand. Critics of psychoanalytic and psychological theory would readily agree with Stanley Hoffman that "it partakes of the fascination of adventure stories: it is the search for the missing clue and the missing link, a search in which everything revealed is treated as a sign of something concealed, and things expressed are deemed the revelation of things repressed."

In contrast, Hoffman prefers to emphasize the centrality of politics and statecraft: "the way in which the leader conceives of and carries out his role as statesman, his relations with and impact on his followers or opponents." From this perspective, the League of Nations failure can be explained in the simpler terms of inept lobbying on Capitol Hill by the president and his aides, coupled with a political tide running against Wilson for a variety of political and international reasons having nothing at all to do with his relationship with his father during adolescence. From Hoffman's point of view, foreign policy leaders are ruled far less by inner demons than by external realities.

Psychological pressures on foreign policy leaders

Washington officials sometimes display psychological vulnerabilities, nevertheless, such as a tendency toward isolation from objective facts about the world, as in President Trump's refusal to believe that he had actually lost the fair and open election of 2020. One psychological danger is sycophancy – blind obedience to a charismatic leader. "In a thousand conference rooms, where the smell of moral sterility is as strong as ether in a hospital corridor," journalists Baker and Peters observed during the Nixon years, "the new courtiers dance to their minuet each day and [government] organizations slip further and further from reality." The Trump Administration was notorious for the president's insistence on extreme loyalty to him that harbored no room for debate or criticism of his worldviews. The end result can be a foreign policy based less on fact than on fantasy.

Another theory, and more readily researched than various psychological theories, is a leader's "operational code," which is made up of his or her fundamental philosophical and instrumental beliefs. Does the leader approach political goals from a moralist-ideological, or a pragmatic and problem-solving, perspective? Does he or she look upon foreign adversaries in "zero-sum" terms (that is, as a life and death struggle with only one winner), or in "positive sum" terms with a more cooperative attitude and a willingness to bargain based on a conviction that nations can cooperate with one another? In the pursuit of global objectives, does the leader believe in the use of armed intervention or in less intrusive instruments of foreign policy? These are vital questions, the answers to which can provide insights into the likely decisions of an official.

Who can deny the importance of individuals in the drama of American foreign policy? Consider this description of relations between high-ranking officials in the Reagan Administration. "Think of someone you really hate," said a foreign policy insider during the Reagan years. "Multiply that by twenty and raise the answer to the fourth power. Then you will have an idea of how [George P.] Shultz and [Caspar] Weinberger [the secretaries of State and Defense, respectively] feel toward one another." According to a senior official in the Reagan Administration, the Assistant Secretary of State for Latin American affairs and a key NSC staff aid "fought like cats and dogs and would not speak to each other." Another observer of this Administration reported that Secretary Shultz "had come to loathe [CIA Director William J.] Casey." No wonder the Administration fell into the disgrace of the Iran-*contra* covert action scandal. In contrast, the foreign policy team assembled by President George H. W. Bush was a model of harmony, and that Administration's foreign policy moved forward more smoothly.

How well individuals relate to one another, and how well they cope with the stresses of their own psychic civil wars, can influence the quality of policymaking. Government is, to a significant degree, a matter of personal relations and bonds of trust. Presidents, legislators, diplomats, bureaucrats, lobbyists – all are made of flesh and blood. They are moved by the often-contradictory emotions of trust and suspicion, love and hate, altruism and avarice, toughness and charity, fatigue, anger, idealism, fear, ambition, pride, zeal, restraint, and all the other feelings that give humanity its character and complexity. How these emotions are handled by officials can be a matter of consequence to America's foreign policy decisions. As John Stuart Mill understood, "The worth of a State, in the long run, is the worth of the individuals composing it."

Notes

On foreign policy and public opinion, see Richard A. Brody, *Assessing the President: The Media Elite Opinion, and Public Support* (Stanford, CA: Stanford University Press, 1991); and Doris A. Graeber, *Mass Media and American Politics*, 7th ed. (Washington, D.C.: CQ Press, 2005). For insights into the relationship between foreign policy and psychology, see Alexander L. George and Juliette L. George, *Woodrow Wilson and Colonel House: A Personality Study* (New York: Dover, 1956); Margaret G. Hermann, ed., *A Psychological Examination of Political Leaders* (New

York: Free Press, 1977); and Harold Lasswell, *Power and Personality* (New York: Norton, 1948). On the Brody and Shapiro research, see Richard A. Brody and Catherine R. Shapiro, "A Reconsideration of the Rally Phenomenon in Public Opinion," in Samuel Long, ed., *Political Behavior Annual*, Vol. 2 (Boulder, CO: Westview, 1989): 77–102; for the Hoffman quote, see his "Heroic Leadership," in Lewis J. Edinger, ed., *Political Leadership in Industrialized Societies* (New York: Wiley, 1967): 109; for commentary on White House sycophancy, see Russell Baker and Charles Peters, "The Prince and His Courtiers," *Washington Monthly* 3 (March 1971): 42–48; and for the troubled personal relationships in the Reagan Administration: Professor Michael Nacht, remarks, Harvard-MIT Summer Program on Nuclear Weapons, as well as John Felton, *Congressional Quarterly Weekly Report* 45 (August 29, 198): 66, and Bob Woodward, *Bush At War* (New York: Simon & Schuster, 2002): 348. The Mill quote is from his *On Liberty*, Harvard Classics, Vol. 25 (New York: Collier, 1901): 212.

PART IV

The instruments of foreign policy

Intelligence collection-and-analysis

America's leaders in the War of Independence were well aware of the vital role intelligence would play in a successful revolutionary struggle. In 1776, the Continental Congress established the nation's first intelligence service, the Committee of Secret Correspondence; and General George Washington, who had his own secret code ("711"), made use of an effective network of spies led by Paul Revere. Perhaps the most famous officer in this network was young Nathan Hale. A graduate of Yale University, moments before being hanged by the British in 1776 for espionage, he declared: "I only regret that I have but one life to lose for my country."

The interest of the constitutional founders in matters of intelligence went well beyond espionage, that is, the secret collection of information by spies. Important, too, was the interpretation of information gathered by the spies, combined with more openly derived information – what modern practitioners call analysis. Benjamin Franklin, among others, energetically encouraged the use of secret operations for yet another objective: to secretly influence other nations toward a favorable regard for American foreign policy objectives – "covert action," in current parlance (examined in Chapter 12).

The integration of U.S. intelligence

The poor sharing and coordination of intelligence prior to Pearl Harbor was a serious flaw that Harry Truman, who followed FDR as president in April of 1945, vowed to address. President Truman was concerned about future surprise attacks against the United States. As well, he was perturbed by the heavy downpour of intelligence reports that fell on his desk every morning from different parts of government, sometimes directly contradicting one another. He preferred to have a single report from a central organization. Most of all, he wanted a more sophisticated intelligence capability to monitor the activities of a rising adversary, the Soviet Union.

On July 26, 1947, the National Security Act established a Central Intelligence Agency. This law placed the CIA, known by insiders as "the Agency," under the control of a new White House structure that would henceforth coordinate American foreign policy: the National Security Council or NSC (Chapter 7). The CIA failed to achieve undisputed dominance over matters of national security intelligence, as its advocates had hoped it would. A deputy director of the CIA, Admiral Rufus Taylor, ruefully described the various intelligence agencies in the late 1960s as little more than a "tribal federation." Strong centrifugal forces in the intelligence system continue to vex policymakers in Washington.

From 1947 to 2004, a Director of Central Intelligence (DCI) led the intelligence agencies and also served as the director of the CIA (D/CIA). Wearing the DCI hat, the director had the primary mission of trying to coordinate information from the different intelligence agencies for presentation to the principal decision-makers in the government – "all-source fusion," or the pooling of information collected from around the world. Absent authority to hire and fire agency heads or shape their budgets, however, the DCI was only the titular head of the intelligence "community." In the aftermath of the 9/11 attacks in 2001, reformers attempted to strengthen the DCI by way of the Intelligence Reform and Terrorism Prevention Act (IRTPA), enacted in 2004.

This law failed to achieve the goal of reformers. The Department of Defense lobbied against a strong national intelligence director, fearful that a civilian spy chief might dilute attention in Washington to military intelligence requirements – an unlikely occurrence, since support to military operations (SMO) will always remain the top U.S. intelligence priority. The office of DCI was given a new name, the Director of National Intelligence (DNI), but the powers of the position over budgets and appointments remained almost as slim as they had been for the DCI. Today, an enfeebled DNI must plead for intelligence sharing, as the cabinet secretaries – especially the Secretary of Defense – resist attempts to erode their authority over intelligence activities within their departments. Two decades after the 9/11 attacks, America still had no true national spymaster.

The structure of intelligence

As with the DCI earlier, just how difficult the job of the DNI is can be appreciated by a look at the way intelligence is structured in the United States. The fragmentation of the U.S. intelligence apparatus is reflected in the sheer number of secret agencies under the DNI's titular leadership: 17 organizations. Nine are military units and they dominate intelligence spending, absorbing over 85 percent of the total U.S. intelligence budget that exceeds US$80 billion a year. Much of this spy funding goes toward the collection-and-analysis of tactical intelligence used by military commanders in the field and admirals at sea, in contrast to broader strategic intelligence used by policy planners in the nation's highest decision councils. A large portion of the overall intelligence budget (a classified amount) supports the work of America's largest espionage organization, the National Security Agency. The NSA, embedded within the framework of the Defense Department as well as the Intelligence Community (IC), has fleets of eavesdropping satellites and ground antennae overseas that are capable of intercepting telephone and e-mail communications in countries around the globe. It is also America's cryptological, or code-breaking, center. While the CIA receives more publicity, in large part because of its controversial involvement in periodic plots to overthrow foreign governments, the NSA and other military organizations comprise the hidden mass of the intelligence iceberg.

America's other military spy agencies include the National Geospatial-intelligence Agency (NGA), which commands the nation's capacity to take photographs of enemy targets by way of sophisticated cameras on satellites and reconnaissance aircraft; the National Reconnaissance Office (NRO), which administers NSA and NGA satellites, from production and launching to their management in space; and the Defense Intelligence Agency (DIA), which analyzes global information gathered on military matters. Four other intelligence units, one in each of the military services, engage in tactical intelligence gathering and analysis; and the newest member of the IC, known as Space Force and created in January of 2021, is dedicated to protecting space as a domain free and open to all nations.

The civilian side of intelligence includes seven agencies within cabinet departments, plus the independent CIA. The seven include the Federal Bureau of Investigation (FBI), located in the Justice Department and responsible for counterterrorism and counterintelligence; the Drug Enforcement Administration (DEA), also in the Department of Justice (DoJ); the Bureau of Intelligence and Research (INR) in the State Department; the Energy Department's intelligence unit, which focuses on tracking nuclear materials worldwide; the Treasury Department's intelligence unit, given the task of tracing the international funding of terrorist organizations; an analytic group within the Department of Homeland Security (DHS); and Coast Guard Intelligence.

Combined, the Intelligence Community adds up to 18 organizations, counting the coordinating Office of the DNI. These entities employ some 200,000 individuals, a large number of whom are contract workers hired temporarily from the private sector. No country, or even empire, throughout history has developed an intelligence apparatus as large and as costly as this set of shadowy organizations. Given the CIA's prominence, it is examined further here as an example of how America's secret agencies are organized and operate.

Inside the CIA

The CIA is now run by the Director of the Central Intelligence Agency (D/CIA). During the Cold War, the precursor of this office – the DCI – had his hands full (no women held the position) just trying to administer the CIA. Even though the Agency is now headed by a D/CIA (since 2004) who doesn't have to worry about community-wide management problems, the challenge of running the CIA remains daunting. In the hallways adjacent to and beneath the D/CIA's suite of offices on the seventh floor of the Agency's headquarters overlooking the Potomac River in Langley, Virginia, are a maze of offices with thousands of analysts, operatives, scientists, clerical assistants, and computer technicians who labor toward the goals of understanding, anticipating, and sometimes shaping world events. The Agency is divided into the office of D/CIA and, under this position, five directorates: Directorate of Operations (DO); Directorate of Science and Technology (DS&T); Directorate of Support (DS); Directorate of Intelligence (DI); and the newly created Directorate of Digital Innovation (DDI).

Directorate of Operations

The largest and most controversial of these units is the Directorate of Operations. About two-thirds of its personnel are engaged in espionage, counterintelligence, and liaison work with intelligence services in allied nations. The rest are assigned to carry out some form of covert action, including paramilitary operations or the secret financing of friendly politicians overseas. The top CIA officer in each country is called the chief of station (COS). Beneath the COS serve the Agency's case officers and their native agents, known as "assets." The CIA places an emphasis on the recruitment of spies abroad living in "hard target" nations, such as North Korea, Iran, Russia, and other dictatorships – a difficult task, because these closed societies have erected formidable defenses (counterintelligence) against America's espionage efforts.

Directorate of Science and Technology

The Directorate of Science and Technology, the smallest of the Agency's directorates, is devoted to the application of technology to espionage. It conducts research and development on gadgetry used by CIA officers and assets in the field, reminiscent of Dr. Q's role in the James Bond movies. The products include everything from advanced lock-picking tools to disguises of all kinds, as well as fake rocks and trees with hollowed out spaces for hiding messages, and even mechanical birds that carry listening devises in their bellies or cameras under their wings as they flap around forbidden foreign territory.

Directorate of Support

The Directorate of Support carries out the Agency's housekeeping chores: hiring, training, worldwide communications and logistics, security, and various other administrative duties – from hanging art in the Agency's hallways to sweeping the floors. It also administers polygraph tests to recruits and, periodically, to employees.

Directorate of Intelligence

The Directorate of Intelligence is where the CIA attempts to make sense of ("analyze" or assess) information about international events and personalities that assets and spy machines (such as satellites and reconnaissance aircraft) have gathered from around the world. It is an intelligence mission to protect the United States by providing its leaders with accurate and timely information about world affairs.

Directorate of Digital Innovation

This new unit is responsible for helping with cyberdefense against foreign hackers who aim at undermining the United States and stealing its secrets (counterintelligence activities), as well as conducting its own cyberattacks against terrorist organizations and other U.S. adversaries (a form of covert action).

The intelligence cycle

The CIA engages in intelligence collection-and-analysis, as well as covert action and counterintelligence. This first mission is fundamental to American foreign policy and is carried out by way of an "intelligence cycle," which the Agency defines as "the process by which information is acquired, converted into intelligence, and made available to policymakers." It has five phases: planning and direction, collection, processing, production and analysis, and dissemination.

Planning and direction

The purpose of the cycle is to provide useful knowledge to leaders in Washington in advance of their decisions. The motto inscribed on the wall at the DNI's headquarters is "Creating Decision Advantage." Major difficulties arise, however, in this seemingly straightforward relationship between the Agency (the producer of knowledge) and the policymakers (the consumers). For example, the informational requirements of policymakers may exceed the capabilities of the CIA, such as the question of exactly how many atomic bombs North Korea has hidden in its underground caverns. Or policymakers may choose to disbelieve or ignore the information provided by the Agency and its companion espionage organizations, as was often the case with President Trump.

Collection

This planet may be but a tiny speck in the universe from a cosmological point of view, but its dimensions are vast for any spy agency trying to keep up with events in the nearly 200 nations of the world. The managers of the intelligence cycle must decide, in consultation with policymakers, which countries to spy on, what kinds of information are most important to gather, and what means of collection is likely to be most effective. The selection of intelligence targets, known as the setting of requirements or "tasking," is a job involving many hands, sometimes even the president. Policymakers might like to know what has occurred, say, within the Ivory Coast over the past two hours, or whether Russia is presently supplying the Syrian regime with attack helicopters to defend against insurgents. In these examples, the policymaker desires "current intelligence" – that is, up-to-the-minute information that is often vital in times of crisis. Or, in contrast, a policymaker might desire instead an in-depth study on a specific subject, accompanied by a long-range prediction. This form of intelligence reporting is known as "research intelligence" or an "estimate," say, a definitive examination of potential leadership succession in China, an analysis of the suspected Iranian nuclear weapons program, or even a topic as narrow as the efficiency of North Korean rocket fuel.

The Intelligence Community relies on three approaches to the gathering of information. Two are covert collection methods: using spies (human intelligence, or "humint" in the intelligence acronym); and using modern technical or machine-based surveillance, especially satellites and drone aircraft (technical intelligence or "techint"). About 90–95 per cent of intelligence material in peacetime, however, is overtly collected from non-secret sources such as foreign newspapers, libraries, radio broadcast, business and industrial reports, or from U.S. Foreign Service officers – open-source intelligence or "osint." As valuable as osint can be, a well-placed humint asset may be able to steal a key document from a safe in the middle of the night, or may overhear foreign leaders discuss impending military operations; and satellites can photograph the number and location of Russian and Chinese missiles. These topics are unlikely to be covered in open newspaper reporting.

Processing

The third step in the intelligence cycle is the least disputatious, but is still difficult. Here the collected information undergoes various refinements for closer study by analysts. Coded data must be decrypted; foreign languages translated into English; satellite photographs interpreted. The purpose is to make the information readable and understandable for the analyst. The major problem during the processing stage is information overload. A related challenge is separating out the meaningful "signals" from all the "noise" that is pulled in by intelligence collection machines and human spies – separating the wheat from the chaff. NSA Director Admiral Noel Gayler complained that he felt as though a "fire hose was held to my mouth," so overwhelming was the deluge of information – useful and useless – gathered by his agency's interceptors.

Analysis

The individuals responsible for the conversion of "raw" (unevaluated) information into "finished" (evaluated) intelligence are called analysts. They are highly educated men and women who are experts on a single country, such as Zaire; on broad topics, such as the flow of petrodollars; or on quite narrow – albeit important – topics, such as the likely leadership succession in Russia or Venezuela. The tools they use are similar to the ones used at universities: computers, library searching, poring over documents, talking with experts, thinking hard about connections they are beginning to notice – like archeologists piecing together an ancient ruin, shard by shard. Within the rubric of current intelligence, preeminent among the reports prepared by the CIA and its companion agencies is the *President's Daily Brief (PDB)*. Longer-range research reports include National Intelligence Estimates (NIEs): a statement of what is going to happen in any country, in any area, in any given situation, as far as possible into the future. As with the *PBD*, the NIE contributes facts and objective interpretations to high-level discussions about how Washington should proceed on the world stage.

Even though the resources devoted to collection-and-analysis is great, the Intelligence Community (like every other human enterprise) will never be free of mistakes, especially in a world that is increasing complex and fragmented. As Richard K. Betts has emphasized: "Some incidence of failure [is] inevitable." He urges a higher "tolerance for disaster" among policymakers. The final phase of the intelligence cycle, dissemination, is also replete with possibilities for error, including the intentional distortion of information – the cardinal sin of intelligence.

Dissemination

Intelligence officers and senior policymakers must talk to each other if the transfer of intelligence is to work properly – not easy, given the frenetic schedules of Washington's decision-makers. Further, as a former senior Agency analyst states, "Many of the consumers are ideologues. It is hard to work with them – especially when we're usually dealing with highly ambiguous data. When consumers criticize our product, it is often on grounds that it fails to support their suppositions." This rejection by policymakers of objective intelligence for their own political reasons, known as the "politicization" of intelligence, became particularly controversial during the Reagan and Trump Administrations. Critics charged DCI William J. Casey, the former presidential campaign manager for Ronald Reagan, with "cooking" (slanting) some intelligence reports to suit the ideological preferences of the White House; or picking out from intelligence findings only those items that supported the policy aspirations of the White House – a selective use of intelligence known as "cherry-picking." And President Trump simply refused to believe many intelligence reports, such as the conclusion that Russian manipulation of the 2016 U.S. presidential election contributed significantly to his victory that year.

Despite all of these challenges, intelligence often provides a reliable foundation for the making of thoughtful foreign policy decisions. The United States will continue to spend considerable resources on expanding and improving these capabilities, especially in the realms of early warning against military, chemical, and biological attacks against the homeland, as well as against cyberattacks.

Notes

On the U.S. intelligence agencies, see David M. Barrett, *The CIA and Congress: The Untold Story from Truman to Kennedy* (Lawrence: University Press of Kansas, 2005); Richard K. Betts, *Enemies of Intelligence:*

Knowledge & Power in American National Security (New York: Columbia University Press, 2007); James R. Clapper, with Trey Brown, *Facts and Fears: Hard Truths from a Life in Intelligence* (New York: Viking, 2018); Rhodri Jeffreys-Jones, *The CIA and American Democracy* (New Haven, CT: Yale University Press, 1989); Robert Jervis, *Why Intelligence Fails: Lessons from the Iranian Revolution and the Iraq War* (Ithaca, NY: Cornell University Press, 2010); Loch K. Johnson, ed., *The Oxford Handbook of National Security Intelligence* (New York: Oxford, 2010); Mark M. Lowenthal, *Intelligence: From Secrets to Policy*, 7th ed. (Washington, D.C.: CQ Press, 2018); and Amy Zegart, *Spying Blind* (Princeton, NJ: Princeton University Press, 2007). For the Gayler quote, see Loch K. Johnson, *A Season of Inquiry: The Senate Intelligence Investigation* (Lexington: University Press of Kentucky, 1985): 83; for the "processing" quote, the author's interview with an NSA official who cited Vice Admiral J. M. McConnell's view (July 14, 1994), Washington, D.C.; for the "tolerance" recommendation, Richard K. Betts, "Analysis, War and Decision: Why Intelligence Failures Are Inevitable," *World Politics* 31 (October 1978): 78; and for the analyst's quote, Arthur S. Hulnick, remarks, Conference on U.S. Intelligence, CIA (June 11, 1984), Virginia.

10 Diplomacy

Diplomacy, from the Greek word *diplomata*, meaning "folded documents," may be defined as the means of representation and negotiation by which nations deal with one another in times of peace; or, stated more simply by Kennan, diplomacy is "the business of communicating between governments." While the job description sounds straightforward, the actual practice of diplomacy is complicated, and with often far-reaching ramifications for a nation – however bland this approach to foreign policy may seem in comparison to sending in the Marines or unleashing the CIA. As the distinguished British statesman Lord Salisbury (1830–1903) once observed, the victories of the diplomat "are made up of a series of microscopic advantages: of a judicious suggestion here, of an opportune civility there, of a wise concession at one moment and a farsighted persistence at another; of sleepless tact, immovable calmness and patience that no folly, on provocation, no blunders can shake." These small steps and intricate compromises, while usually lacking in drama, can move a nation toward momentous and sometimes dangerous commitments abroad. Further, one person's "wise concession at the one moment" may be another's unacceptable "appeasement."

An approach known as coercive diplomacy can be important, too. This policy involves signaling to other nations that a diplomatic settlement may be in their best interests, since the alternative could mean the introduction of military force into the equation. In this vein Walter F. Mondale, vice president for Jimmy Carter, has written: "I've always been proud that our administration never started a war or dropped a bomb. But I've also believed that our ability to do both helped us change minds, tame rivals, and promote human rights – as well as prevent deadly attacks on Americans." Similarly, CIA Director Leon Panetta of the Obama Administration (and later Secretary of Defense) noted in 2010 that the Taliban extremists supporting Al Qaeda were unlikely to enter into negotiations with the governments of Afghanistan or America "unless they're convinced that the United States is going to win and that they're going to be defeated." The sword, or the threat of the sword, must sometimes prepare the way for the dove of peace.

The making of international agreements

As introduced in Chapter 6, the United States uses three prominent forms of formal diplomatic agreements with other nations: the treaty, the statutory agreement, and the executive agreement. Treaties are required by Article II, Section 2 of the Constitution to have the support (the "advice and consent") of two-thirds of those members of the Senate present and voting. On any important treaty quite likely all 100 members will be present, so the executive branch must muster at least 67 votes. The statutory agreement involves legislative authority, too; but, instead of an extraordinary two-thirds approval in the Senate, which is difficult to achieve on contentious issues, this procedure requires an easier majority vote – but in both chambers, that is, 51 senators and 218 members of the House (if every member is present and voting). Easiest of all for a president is to bypass the Congress altogether by way of an executive agreement, entered into by the executive branch with another country without advice and consent from the Senate or counsel from the House of Representatives.

Increasingly, members of Congress began to believe in the 1960s that executive branch administrations were resorting to executive agreements, proclamations, and other unilateral actions as a way of circumventing their participation in the formulation of America's formal international commitments. Well in advance of the Vietnam War era, "diplomacy was conducted as often as possible to avoid formal congressional involvement," conceded a former U.S. ambassador. Especially worrisome to lawmakers were secret pacts with other nations signed by the White House or the bureaucracy and never revealed to Congress, including verbal "promises" and "understandings" – smile-and-wink deals that were seldom committed to parchment.

In the early stages of the Cold War (1945 to 1972), for example, the overwhelming number – almost 87 percent – of all U.S. agreements were statutory in form, that is, they involved bicameral legislative as well as executive branch approval. In contrast, executive agreements and treaties accounted for only 7 percent and 6 percent of all the agreements, respectively. These figures indicate that Congress has been included in the agreement-making process; indeed, lawmakers participated in the overwhelming percentage of these early Cold War international agreements, by providing House and Senate authority through the statutory agreement process. These data show, too, that the statutory agreement has largely replaced the treaty as the primary method for the making of U.S. commitments abroad.

More recently, statutory agreements remain the dominant form of international commitment by the United States, although some nations prefer from time to time that the United States use the treaty process as a signal that a new pact is of highest importance and will endure. There continue to be times, as well, when Congress has been completely shut out of deliberations over significant commitments abroad, as presidents and bureaucrats rely on executive agreements to carry out foreign policy without legislative "interference."

The hidden side of diplomacy

In a study released in 1972, members of the Senate Foreign Relations Committee reported: "As the committee has discovered, there have been numerous agreements contracted with foreign governments in recent years, particularly agreements of a military nature, which remain wholly unknown to Congress and to the people." A central question is: were these obligations of sweeping significance? For an answer, one must turn to a more qualitative review of the military commitments discovered by members of the SFRC. The evidence found by the Committee revealed that, on occasion, these kinds of agreements have proven to be controversial and costly. For instance, executive agreements to place U.S. troops and weapons abroad, known as forward deployment, can add up to an expensive portion of the Pentagon's budget and, even more disquieting, can lead the United States into war.

Some lawmakers believe that the executive branch has sought out the advice and consent of the Senate primarily for diplomatic initiatives that are only of little substantive importance. For more important commitments overseas, the White House has turned to executive agreements – what a U.S. diplomat has referred to as a "precarious and ephemeral" way of conducting foreign policy. Senator Dick Clark (D-Iowa) railed on the Senate floor that "the treaty form has been used for a shrimp agreement with Brazil, an agreement on the conservation of polar bears, and an agreement regarding the uninhabited coral reefs in the Caribbean." Other treaties have dealt with the recovery of lost archaeological objects in Mexico, an increase in membership of the International Atomic Energy Board from 25 to 35, and the international classification of industrial designs. "If an agreement involves a very minor matter on the allocation of radio waves with Mexico, it is presented as a treaty," once observed the longest-serving chairman of the Senate Foreign Relations Committee, J. William Fulbright (D-Arkansas), in agreement with Senator Clark. "If it is a tax matter with Luxembourg involving equal treatment, it is a treaty. But if it involves circumstance likely to result in war, it is an executive agreement, kept a secret and then presented to Congress as a *fait accompli*."

Senators Clark and Fulbright had reason for concern. Although 43 of the 142 executive agreements dealing with military policy were routine and minor from 1946 to 1974, addressing such topics as the establishment of a practice bombing range in West Germany and reciprocal air rights with Canada for rescue operations, a striking number involved major obligations abroad. Seventy percent (99 of 142) of the military agreements during this time period were important enough to have warranted closer scrutiny by the legislative branch. Several involved the establishment of overseas bases. The exclusion of a role for Congress in the making of such commitments has been a source of tension between the executive and legislative branches ever since these early Cold War years, as the president asserts authority under the commander-in-chief clause and the Congress sometimes resists what it perceives as unwise agreements entered into without the benefit of rigorous legislative review. As the following examples illustrate, presidents have indeed abused the privilege of signing executive agreements in the past and there is no reason to believe they will refrain from doing so in the future.

Military agreements

A number of case examples disclose how the misuse of executive agreements can have a pernicious effect on American foreign policy. Thailand offers a telling illustration.

Thailand

In 1962, Secretary of State Dean Rusk and the Foreign Minister of Thailand, Thanat Khoman, issued a joint statement in which Rusk expressed "the firm intention of the United States to aid Thailand, its ally and historic friend, in resisting Communist aggression and subversion." This language went far beyond the wording of the treaty signed by members of the Southeast Asia Treaty Organization (SEATO), which provided only that the member nations would "consult" in times of military peril and act to meet the common danger in accordance with their own "constitutional processes." The end result of the Rusk-Khoman joint communiqué was to convert SEATO's collective security arrangement into a bilateral U.S.-Thai defense pact. Under the new relationship, the U.S. Military Assistance Program (MAP) for Thailand shot upward from US$24 million in 1960 to US$88 million in 1962. Further, in 1966 the two nations entered into negotiations over a secret contingency agreement, signed in 1969. This arrangement promised joint action in the event of a conventional military attack against Thailand. The agreement also paid special bonuses to Thai combat troops in Vietnam – in essence the hiring of mercenaries to fight in this civil war on America's behalf. Through a communiqué and a secret executive agreement, the original intent of a solemn treaty approved by the Senate, SEATO, had been significantly altered.

Laos

In another example from the 1960s, the executive branch launched a wide array of secret military and CIA paramilitary operations in Laos, without any written agreements whatsoever. Everything was based on "oral understandings" that, according to a Department of State official, were just as binding as written ones. Among the commitments made in this manner were the placement of American spotters in combat zones.

During hearings, a Senate subcommittee tried to find out how all this had come to pass:

Subcommittee counsel: Under what authority are the American personnel in Laos there?
State Department official: They are there under the executive authority of the president.

The dangers of diplomacy by executive fiat

These cases, and many similar examples, suggest a number of conclusions about the conduct of American diplomacy. First, U.S. military commitments abroad have often been based on slender reeds of authority. While the oral understandings with the government of Laos may represent an extreme illustration, various other secret letters, communiqués, and agreements reflect a foreign policy dominated by anonymous bureaucrats, closed doors, and confidential covenants. Further, sometimes America's diplomatic obligations are stretched far beyond the original intent of Congress, or even the White House – a development known as creeping commitments. This distortion occurs as executive branch officials seek to fill in the details once a broad agreement is reached. These "auxiliary arrangements" can assume a bewildering variety of forms, including memoranda of understanding, exchanges of notes, exchanges of letters, technical addendums, protocols, the *note verbale*, the *aide-mémoire*, agreed minutes, joint communiqués, joint military plans, military assistance programs, and the stationing of troops overseas.

Constitutional diplomacy

In 1972, the Senate took a major step toward instituting tighter legislative control over international agreements. Out of a sense of despair regarding the inability of lawmakers even to find out what commitments the executive branch had been making overseas by executive agreement, especially in Indochina, Senator Clifford Case (R-New Jersey) introduced legislation to remove this blind spot. He sought to guarantee that Congress had access to information on all of America's foreign commitments. To this end, the Senate passed the Case Act by an emphatic vote of 81-to-0. Representative Clement Zablocki (D-Wisconsin) introduced the same measure in the House and, six months later, the proposal passed in that chamber, too, by a wide majority. On August 22, 1972, Richard M. Nixon – faced by a united Congress prepared to override a presidential veto – signed the Case-Zablocki Act into law. Henceforth, the State Department would have to report to Congress on all international agreements under negotiation by the executive branch.

In 1978, Senator Clark brought forth a much stronger proposal to ensure that the executive branch kept Congress in the loop on international agreements: the Treaty Powers Resolution. This initiative expressed a sense of the Senate that any "significant" international agreement should be cast as a treaty and submitted to senators for their advice and consent. Section 4 of the resolution bore sharp teeth: if the executive failed to submit an agreement that senators had decided (by a simple majority vote) should have been forwarded to their chamber as a treaty, then the Senate rules would declare it henceforth out of order "to consider any bill or joint resolution or any amendment thereto, or any report of a committee of conference, which authorizes or provides budget authority to implement such international agreement." The congressional money spigots would be shut off for the disputed agreement until the Senate had an opportunity to consider the proposal. The Clark proposal was chiefly a finger-shaking exercise by the SFRC aimed at the executive branch. A majority of the Senate proved unwilling to endorse this intrepid challenge to executive agreements, feeling that the point had been made without formal legislation.

Usually, the executive branch views the statutory agreement as somewhat easier to negotiate on Capitol Hill, since the required approval standard is a simple majority vote in both houses of Congress, as opposed to an extraordinary two-thirds Senate majority vote. In 2002, for example, the second Bush Administration preferred to submit a nuclear arms reduction agreement with Russia as a statutory agreement. The Senate complained vociferously, however, and on this occasion the Administration recanted and submitted the agreement for review through the formal treaty process. The Senate approved the Treaty of Moscow.

Diplomacy's far reach

Agreements with other countries have often been precursors to overt or covert military intervention abroad by the United States. This is why, in the wake of the war in Vietnam, lawmakers have come to believe that Congress has a major stake in America's diplomatic initiatives. "If you've got children or grandchildren who might have to go [to war]," Robert C. Byrd (D-West Virginia), the Senate Majority Leader, once observed, "you'd feel much better with Congress being brought in, than leaving it to one man." During the 1970s, Senator Hubert H. Humphrey (D-Minnesota) warned Secretary of State Cyrus Vance of the Carter Administration as he prepared to depart on a trip to the Middle East: "Don't make any commitments until you've been back here [to Capitol Hill] – not even smiling ones." Most lawmakers and the public understand the need for privacy and secrecy during negotiations with other countries. They also understand, though, that democracy and the Constitution require broader participation than just the White House in the great decisions of diplomacy that can determine the fate of the American people.

Notes

On the topic of diplomacy, see Gordon A. Craig and Felix Gilbert, eds., *The Diplomats: 1919–1939* (Princeton, NJ: Princeton University Press, 1953); Abba Eban, *The New Diplomacy* (New York: Random House, 1983); Amy M. Gilbert, *Executive Agreements and Treaties, 1946–1973* (New York: Thomas-Newell, 1973); Michael J. Glennon, *Constitutional Diplomacy* (Princeton, NJ: Princeton University Press, 1990); Fred C. Ikle, *How Nations Negotiate* (New York: Harper & Row, 1964); Loch K. Johnson, *The Making of International Agreements: Congress Confronts the Executive* (New York: New York University Press, 1984); Henry A. Kissinger, *Diplomacy* (New York: Simon & Schuster, 1994); David D. Newsom, *Diplomacy and the American Democracy* (Bloomington: Indiana University Press, 1988); Sir Harold Nicolson, *Diplomacy* (London: Thornton Butterworth, 1939); and Charles W. Whalen Jr., *The House and Foreign Policy* (Chapel Hill: University of North Carolina Press, 1982). For the Kennan quote, see Norman J. Padelford and George A. Lincoln,

The Dynamics of International Politics (New York: Macmillan, 1962): 340; on Salisbury, British scholar Frank Adams, e-mail to the author (December 21, 1988); for Panetta, see his remarks, *This Week*, ABC News (June 27, 2010); for the ambassador's remarks, see Newsome, *Diplomacy and the American Democracy*: 41; for the SFRC report, see "Transmittal of Executive Agreements to Congress," *Senate Report No. 92-591* (January 19, 1972): 3–4; on the "precarious" nature of executive agreements, the diplomat is Kurt Campbell, now retired, quoted by Robin Wright, "The Seven Pillars of Biden's Foreign Policy," *The New Yorker* (November 11, 2020), and Senator Clark's remarks are in the *Congressional Record* (June 28, 1978): 59996; for Fulbright's observation, see John C. Stennis and J. William Fulbright, *The Role of Congress in Foreign Policy* (Washington, D.C.: American Enterprise Institute, 1971): 83; the exchange on Laos is from "Kingdom of Laos," *Hearings*, SFRC, Part 6 (1970); and Senator Byrd was quoted by *The New York Times* (September 21, 1983): A3, and Senator Humphrey, remark, *Briefing on the Middle East*, SFRC (February 11, 1977).

11 War

The war power – that is, the actual or potential use of overt military force – is the most extreme and hazardous means for the pursuit of foreign policy objectives, especially given the presence of WMD in several countries around the world. The core existential reality in the nuclear age is that nations possessing nuclear weapons can annihilate one another utterly. A motif in this book is the question of how well America's constitutional framework continues to fit the needs of contemporary foreign policy. No topic reveals more emphatically than war-making the disputes that accompany the Constitution's fundamental philosophy of institutional power-sharing.

Uses of the war powers

Since 1798, the United States has been involved in more than 200 military actions overseas. Congress has formally declared war in only five of these instances: the war with Great Britain in 1812, Mexico in 1846, Spain in 1998, and the two world wars. On more than 60 other occasions, lawmakers have given some other form of legislative approval for fighting abroad, from the appropriation of monies to the passage of resolutions in support of war. Fully 140 engagements, the overwhelming majority, were the result, though, of a decision reached by the president without the imprimatur of lawmakers.

During and since the Cold War, the U.S. military arsenal has been comprised of an imposing array of nuclear and conventional weapons. Since the end of the Cold War, the United States has taken up conventional arms to fight terrorism in the Middle East (Iraq), Southwest Asia (Afghanistan and Pakistan), Northern Africa, and a number of other locations around the world. The Authorization for Use of Military Force (AUMF), enacted by Congress a few days after 9/11 to fight back at Al Qaeda and its Taliban hosts in Afghanistan, provided the president with authority to arrest or kill anyone suspected of committing or assisting in terrorist assaults involving the United States, or who provided a safe haven to the attackers. This statute authorized the war in Afghanistan and the killing of Osama bin Laden. While sympathetic to the need for fighting terrorism, critics have questioned the open-ended character of the AUMF authority, which seems to give the president boundless rights – in advance – to engage in military operations in every corner of the globe.

During the Cold War, a goal of "deterrence" – warding off enemies – was meant to be achieved by threatening a massive, retaliatory nuclear attack against the Soviet Union or China, if their troops dared to invade Western Europe, South Korea, Japan, or other territories considered important to America's security interests and economic prosperity. By 1957, the Soviets had achieved a capacity to strike the United States with long-range, nuclear-tipped missiles. A situation of mutual deterrence had come into existence. Both superpowers were able to shield against the outbreak of a strike against their homelands, or their major allies, through this threat of mutual assured destruction (MAD). This prospect of mutual suicide stood as a potent psychological barrier against the outbreak of another global war between the superpowers.

Even at lower levels of conflict, in the aftermath of the Vietnam debacle President Reagan's leading advisers began to express a sense of caution about use of the war power. This new restraint was evident in Secretary of Defense Caspar Weinberger's so-called six commandments:

- The military action had to involve vital national interests
- The United States must intend to win
- The operation had to have clear-cut political-military objectives
- These objectives had to be subjected to a continual reassessment
- The American people had to be in support
- All alternatives to the use of overt force had to have been tried first and found wanting

The Secretary said his intention was to "sound a note of caution" against the rash use of military force.

Subsequently, Chairman of the Joint Chiefs of Staff Colin L. Powell (later Secretary of State in the second Bush Administration) argued that if America were to go to war, the nation should use overwhelming force to win quickly. A more recent JCS Chairman, Admiral Mike Mullen of the second Bush and the Obama Administrations, backed away from this Powell Doctrine, however, on grounds that it smacked of recklessness. The military, he argued in 2010, "must not try to use force only in an overwhelming capacity, but in the proper capacity, and in a precise and principled manner."

Weapons of war in the nuclear age

Tactical nuclear and conventional weaponry

A nation's tactical nuclear capability encompasses weapons that rely on a nuclear reaction (the splitting of atoms, which releases energy) for their destructive force, but are designed for relatively small targets on the battlefield. Some, though – so-called theater nuclear weapons – can deliver a punch ("yield") greater than the bombs dropped on Hiroshima and Nagasaki. During the Cold War, these weapons varied in size from backpack warheads (for use by the infantry, say, to stop a tank) and howitzer shells (with a range of 20 miles or so), to the NATO Lance battlefield-support missile and its Warsaw Pact Frog-7 counterpart (with ranges of 80 and 43 miles, respectively). In contrast, conventional armaments rely on non-nuclear technology: everything from M-16 rifles to the blast effect of chemical reactions like TNT. This distinction can sometimes be artificial, however, since the power of some high-yield conventional weapons is barely distinguishable from low-yield tactical nuclear weapons in the damage they inflict.

The strategic nuclear triad

The strategic deterrent capability of the United States rests on a nuclear "triad," which is based on three types of weaponry: ground-based ICBMs; airborne intercontinental bombers; and sea-based submarine-launched ballistic missiles or SLBMs. A concern about the ground-based leg stems from the vulnerability of America's ICBMs to enemy attack, since these missiles are stationary targets inside silos that dot mainly the western and midwestern landscape of the United States. Although they are hidden underground and sheltered by heavy layers of concrete, foreign spies know where these missiles are; and foreign missiles can pack a sufficient wallop to destroy them.

In this regard, the bomber leg of the triad has a special advantage. During the Cold War, several U.S. bombers were constantly in the air and ready to head for Russia over the Artic Circle; and about 30 percent of this force was always on alert and would probably have been able to lift off their runways and survive a Soviet first strike. Yet, even when airborne, they are relatively slow-moving targets for enemy aircraft and missilry.

The submarine leg is the least vulnerable system. Hidden deep beneath the ocean's surface, *each* of America's nuclear submarines – numbering close to 40 – during the latter decades of the Cold War carried more destructive power than the combined total detonated during every war fought since the dawn of humanity. Moreover, submarines are difficult for enemies to locate and, even if found, they are hard to attack. Their major shortcoming is the difficulty of communicating to a vessel deeply submerged in the ocean.

The distribution of nuclear weapons across the triad for the United States and Russia in 2012 is shown below:

	United States	*Russia*
ICBMs	500	1,087
SLBMs	1,152	528
Bombers	300	820
Total	1,952	2,435

Command and control

The task of disseminating information and orders from decision-makers to their military commanders in the field is referred to in military circles as command-control-communications-and-intelligence (C^3I). In the modern era, these linkages have presented some alarming scenarios. During the Cold War, for example, computer chips were known to have failed in America's early warning system, giving false signals that a Soviet attack was underway. Once, what seemed to be a sky filled with Soviet missiles that lit up U.S. defense radar screens proved to be merely a gaggle of geese. On another occasion, a bevy of swans was mistaken for a squadron of Soviet MIG aircraft. Moreover, sensitive communications networks can be jammed by an adversary, say, with heavy-metal rock music at 300 decibels.

A core C^3I challenge is how to protect U.S. command posts. One can conceive of a well-coordinated, simultaneous enemy strike against the White House, the Congress, the Pentagon, and other command centers that would deprive the United States of its top leadership in time of war – a swift military stroke referred to as a nuclear decapitation. In defense against this battle scenario, the United States has fashioned various safeguards. One method has been the establishment of DUCs (deep underground centers) where the National Command Authority (NCA) – the nation's top political and military leaders – can hide from the down-pour of enemy missiles. Moreover, caves have been constructed for this purpose in the mountains of Maryland, in the Virginia countryside, and in Colorado at the NORAD (North American Defense) headquarters near Colorado Springs. In an alert condition indicating an imminent enemy attack or one already under way (Defense Condition One, or "DefCon 1"), the NCA is expected to rush to pre-designated locations – the back-yard of the White House is one – to be whisked away by helicopters into their mountain refuges.

Another possibility is to go aloft. The president has a specially equipped airplane, officially known as the National Emergency Airborne Command Post or NEACAP (pronounced "kneecap"), designed to serve as a head-quarters in time of nuclear war. With America under attack, however, whether the president and top-level staff would have time to board the custom-built Boeing 747 stationed at Andrews Air Force Base in Maryland is problematic. Further, this airplane would be a high-priority target for a surprise submarine-launched missile attack in an enemy's decapitation strategy.

The effects of nuclear weapons

When triggered, nuclear weapons have multiple effects, from the release of intense heat and high winds (the blast effect) to radiation and severe atmospheric disturbances. The immediate consequences of a nuclear explosion are devastating, as witnessed in the dropping of atomic bombs on Japan in 1945. The bombs that obliterated Hiroshima and Nagasaki were mere firecrackers compared to the colossal megaton yields of contemporary nuclear weaponry. Half of the deaths in the target area would come from the release of thermal energy, 35 percent from the blast wave, and 15 percent from the ionized radiation – with the latter lingering for decades. Since the primary enemy targets are usually military bases, weapons silos, and warships (a "counterforce" targeting strategy) or industrial and communications centers (a city, population-oriented "countervalue" targeting strategy), the blast effect is a particularly important consideration for strategists.

The electromagnetic pulse (EMP) associated with nuclear explosions would also have profound consequences in the waging of modern warfare. These atmospheric disturbances can disrupt or paralyze all communications, radar operations, and early warning systems, in the case of a first ("preemptive") strike by an enemy.

Nor can one dismiss the possibility of a nuclear winter that could descend over the planet in the aftermath of a major nuclear war. Using computer modeling, American scientists have estimated that even a limited nuclear war could have catastrophic effects on climate if cities were targeted. Soot from burning buildings would rise into the atmosphere and block out the sun's rays. Even without the descent of a long "nuclear winter," the post-attack conditions that followed a nuclear war would be decidedly grim. Medical supplies would be destroyed, and a high number of physicians and nurses would be killed or incapacitated. Preceding the possible freezing of the earth would first come its scorching and sterilization with the initial impact of the nuclear warheads. From a psychological perspective, the populations of the target nations would experience profound and widespread depression. The United States and the enemy who attacked it would be thrown back into a medieval setting.

Another challenge that confronts nations today is the possibility of chemical, biological, and radiological (CBR) attacks. Biological weapons might incorporate the use of smallpox virus or anthrax against targets; chemical weapons could use sarin, a highly lethal nerve gas; and radiological weapons rely on the spewing of radioactive materials around a target, perhaps by detonating a canister of enriched uranium or plutonium with an old-fashioned TNT explosive. These forms of weaponry are easier for adversaries to manufacture than "nukes," and are easier to hide as well from the prying eyes of U.S. intelligence agencies. Many experts on modern weaponry believe that a biological attack is much more likely than a nuclear attack, and – the nuclear-winter scenario aside – every bit as devastating.

Levels of military funding

In 2020, the United States spent over US$700 billon on defense, equivalent to more than 40 percent of the world's defense expenditures – for a nation that is about 4.6 percent of the world's population. This figure surpasses what every other major nation spends on defense *combined*. In addition to the ever-present military-industrial-intelligence complex within the United States, much of the recent defense spending has been fueled by America's dual wars in Iraq and Afghanistan. They have cost upwards of US$6 trillion so far – the most expensive conflicts in U.S. history, surpassing even the Second World War. No wonder historian Ernest R. May referred to Washington, D.C., as more of a military headquarters than a national capital.

War Powers Resolution

The struggle between the branches for control over the war power in the modern era came to a climax in 1973 with the passage of the War Powers Resolution (WPR). This law states that the use of American troops abroad should rely on the "collective judgment of both the Congress and the President." This principle, as constitutional scholar Louis Fisher observes, "is the dominant lesson of the past four decades." In a similar vein, Professor Eugene Rostow, known for his support of a strong presidency, concluded nonetheless that "if the President and the executive branch cannot persuade Congress and the public that a policy is wise, it should not be pursued."

The WPR requires that the president "in every possible instance shall consult with Congress" before introducing armed forces "into hostilities or into situations where imminent involvement in hostilities is clearly indicated by the circumstances." It further mandates a report to Congress within 48 hours regarding any deployment of U.S. into "hostilities" or a region where hostilities are imminent, as well as when forces "equipped for combat" are sent into a foreign nation; or when forces are deployed that "substantially enlarge" the number of combat-equipped U.S. troops in a foreign territory.

Moreover, the WPR permitted Congress to force the withdrawal of U.S. troops from a region at any time by a concurrent resolution, that is, by a simple majority vote in both chambers – without the need for the president's signature or possible veto. (This provision, though, was nullified by a Supreme Court decision in 1983, *U.S.* v. *Chadha*, on grounds that such a "legislative veto" was unconstitutional.) The Resolution further stipulated that if the Congress refused to formally endorse, by majority votes in both chambers, the president's use of force within 60 days of the initial report, the president *had to* withdraw the U.S. troops. Congress is permitted by the Resolution to grant a 30-day extension, if necessary, to assure an orderly and safe exit. Senator Jacob Javits (R-New York), the Resolution's chief architect, observed after its adoption that "at long last Congress is determined to recapture the awesome power to make war." The WPR, though, has been dogged by controversy. Presidents have sometimes simply ignored several of its provisions. The *Mayaguez* rescue operation in 1975, and U.S. military support to NATO in Libya in 2011, offer illustrations.

Mayaguez rescue

In an unsuccessful attempt to rescue American merchant sailors aboard the vessel *Mayaguez*, captured by Cambodian forces in May 1975, President Gerald R. Ford reported to Congress under the WPR, thereby starting the 60-day clock. The president failed, however, to consult with a single member of Congress in advance of the decision. Leading lawmakers were simply "informed" beforehand through a brief presidential report. Representative Clement Zablocki stated at the time, "Clearly it was not the intention of the Congress [via the WPR] to be merely informed of decisions made." Further, Senator Thomas Eagleton (D-Missouri) complained with heavy sarcasm that "all the President has to do is make a telephone call ... and say, 'The boys are on the way. I think you should know' ... Consultation!"

Moreover, the official reports from President Ford and his successors in compliance with the WPR have been skimpy at best. As a study by Barbara Hinkson Craig concluded: "The reports ... are one- to two-page letters that proffer less information than might be gleaned from reading newspaper coverage of the events. Indeed, the report on the *Mayaguez* operation made no mention of the number of casualties [41 Marines lost their lives in this attempt to rescue 39 U.S. merchant sailors], or the fact that the [U.S.] bombing of a military airfield occurred after the ship and crew were already in custody."

Libya and NATO

The Obama Administration argued that providing air support and intelligence for a NATO mission against Libya was not really a matter of being involved in hostilities, because the president never dispatched U.S. ground troops into the fighting. It was, therefore, irrelevant to notify Congress about the operation through the WPR procedure. Yet U.S. warplanes struck at Libyan air defenses about 60 times, and the Obama Administration used drones to fire missiles at Libyan forces about 30 times. Further, the president ignored the most significant WPR provision: obtaining approval from Congress to keep a military presence in the war zone. Yale University law professor Bruce Ackerman accused the Administration of "undermining a key legal check on arbitrary presidential power ... [and] allowing the trivialization of the War Powers Act." Another constitutional authority, Louis Fisher, pointed to the key principle that should have guided the Libya case: "Other than repelling sudden attack and protecting American lives overseas, presidents may not take the country from a state of peace to a state of war without seeking and obtaining congressional authority."

In addition, at times presidents have skirted the War Powers Resolution altogether, by resorting to CIA covert paramilitary warfare. America's secret foreign policy is the focus of the next chapter.

Notes

On war-making controversies, see: Richard K. Betts, *American Force: Dangers, Delusions, and Dilemmas in National Security* (New York: Columbia University Press, 2012); Freeman J. Dyson, *Weapons and Hope* (New York: Harper & Row, 1984); Max Hastings, *Vietnam: An Epic Tragedy, 1945–1975* (New York: HarperCollins, 2018); and Jonathan Schell, *The Fate of the Earth* (New York: Knopf, 1982). On Weinberger, Powell, and Mullen, see respectively: Bernard E. Trainor, "Weinberger on Persian Gulf," *The New York Times* (October 9, 1987): A20; Colin Powell, "U.S. Forces: Challenges Ahead," *Foreign Affairs* 71 (Winter 1992/1993): 32–45; and Thom Shanker, "Joint Chiefs Chairman Readjusts Principles on Use of Force," *The New York Times* (March 4, 2011): A14. On a nuclear winter, P. R. Ehrlich et al., "The Long-Term Biological Consequences of a Nuclear War," *Science* 222 (December 23, 1983): 145–149. For the May quote, see his "The U.S. Government: A Legacy of the Cold War," *Diplomatic History* 16 (Spring 1992): 270; and for the Fisher and Rostow remarks, see respectively: "Why Congress Passed the War Powers Resolution," Conference Paper, Center for Law and National Security, School of Law, University of Virginia, Charlottesville (September 23, 1988): 23; and "Searching for Kennan's Grand Design," *Yale Law Journal* 87 (1978): 1536. For the Zablocki and Eagleton observations, see respectively: John H. Sullivan, *Hearings, The War Powers Resolution*, Committee on Foreign Affairs, U.S. House of Representatives (1982): 219; and *Congressional Record* (November 7, 1982): 219. For the quote from the *Mayaguez* study, see Barbara Hinkson Craig, "The Power to Make War: Congress' Search for an Effective Role," *Journal of Policy Analysis and Management* 1 (1981): 324; and for the Ackerman and Fisher quotes, see respectively: "Legal Acrobatics, Illegal War," *The New York Times* (June 21, 2011): A27; and "Parsing the War Power," *National Law Journal* (July 4, 2011). The figures on the nuclear triad are from the *Bulletin of the Atomic Scientists* (March–April 2012).

12 Covert action

In the United States, covert action (CA) is sometimes referred to as the "quiet option" by officials inside the CIA, the organization relied upon by the White House to plan and implement this concealed instrument of foreign policy. The phrase is drawn from the debatable assumption that this approach to foreign policy is less likely to be noisy and obtrusive than sending in a Marine brigade. While sometimes this is true, there was nothing quiet about the Cuban Bay of Pigs fiasco in 1961; and today's "covert" CIA drone attacks in Pakistan are routinely discussed in the newspapers and on television. Another label for covert action is the "third option" – a choice for the president between diplomacy, on the one hand, and overt warfare, on the other hand. Still another favorite euphemism in Washington for covert action is the phrase "special activities." In 1991, Congress crafted a formal statutory definition of covert action as "an activity or activities of the United States Government to influence political, economic, or military conditions abroad, where it is intended that the role of the United States Government will not be apparent or acknowledged publicly."

Giving history a push

Covert action is nothing less than a nation's attempt to change the course of world events through the use of secret operations against other countries, terrorist groups, or factions – "giving history a push," in the words of a senior CIA operative. During the Cold War, the main concern of the CIA's Directorate of Operations (DO) was, according to one of its chiefs, "the global challenge of communism ... to be confronted whenever and wherever it seemed to threaten our interests." Whether such targets as Iran (1953), Guatemala (1954), Angola (1975), and Chile (1958–1973) qualified as threatening is a matter of debate. Critics find the arguments for some CIA interventions a stretch. For example, with respect to Nicaragua, a prime target for U.S. covert action during the 1980s, the German Nobel laureate in literature, Günter Grass, asked plaintively: "How impoverished must a country be before it is not a threat to the U.S. government?" Frank Church, who led a Senate inquiry into the subject of covert action in 1975, concluded that America's "targets were leaders of small, weak countries that could not possibly threaten the United States."

Methods of covert action

Covert action became a central preoccupation of officials within the Agency and the White House immediately after the CIA was created in 1947. This secret approach to American foreign policy has taken four major forms over the years: propaganda ("perception management," in the amusing CIA euphemism); political manipulation; economic disruption; and paramilitary (PM) operations or, in plain language, secret warfare.

Propaganda

No form of covert action is used more extensively than secret propaganda. To augment the flow of official information from Washington, D.C., and U.S. embassies around the world, the CIA releases a floodtide of supportive material – some 70 to 80 items a day were inserted into foreign media outlets during the Cold War – distributed through its vast underground network of "media assets." These individuals include reporters, newspaper and magazine editors, television producers, bloggers, and other social media specialists – the whole range of media. Whatever the White House and the State Department may be communicating openly to the world at any given time, the Agency will likely be advancing the same themes through its covert channels, say, during the Reagan Administration, the pernicious influence of the KGB on the peace movement in Western Europe, or, today, the dangers to democracy posed by Al Qaeda and other terrorist organizations.

In addition, the CIA uses its media assets to promote or denigrate foreign political leaders, depending on whether or not these individuals are likely to support the interests of the United States. A classic example is the Agency's endeavor, under orders from Presidents Eisenhower, Johnson, and Nixon, to oppose Chile's socialist president, Salvador Allende. Once released, the CIA's propaganda cannot be bottled up or directed to only one spot on the globe, as one might apply an antiseptic to a sore. Rather, it is free to drift here and there, and even back to the United States. This can lead to "blow-back" or "replay," whereby disinformation aimed at enemies overseas can find its way back home to deceive America's own citizens.

Political covert action

Political covert action takes the form of secret financial aid to friendly politicians and bureaucrats abroad: bribes, if one wishes to put a harsh light on the practice, or stipends to advance the cause of democracy, if one prefers a rosier interpretation. Whatever one calls this assistance ("King George's cavalry" is the expression favored by the British intelligence service, MI6), the record is clear that the United States has secretly provided substantial sums of money to various pro-U.S. political parties, leaders, and would-be leaders around the globe. A favored recipient during the Cold War was the Christian Democratic Party in Italy, which contested elections regularly with the Italian Communist Party (which relied on clandestine funding from the KGB).

Economic covert action

With economic covert action, the Agency attempts when ordered by the White House to disrupt the economies of America's enemies through secret means. In one instance during the Kennedy years, the CIA planned to damage Cuban-Soviet relations by lacing sugar bound from Havana to Moscow with an unpalatable, though harmless, chemical substance. After three NSC meetings on this and related topics, the president rejected the idea and had the 14,125 bags of sugar confiscated before they left for the Soviet Union. During its various anti-Allende activities, the Agency adopted several measures to disrupt the Chilean economy. By heightening the level of unrest under the Allende regime (which had been democratically elected by the people of Chile), Washington hoped that local military forces would decide to strip the president of office.

The CIA provided funding to groups involved in strike tactics, especially within the trucking industry, in an attempt to impede the flow of commerce inside the country. Later in Latin America, as part of the Reagan Administration's efforts to overthrow the Nicaraguan government in the 1980s, the CIA-backed *contras* carried out a range of attacks against the economy, including the mining of piers in the nation's harbors to discourage international shipping, as well as the blowing up of power lines throughout the countryside.

Paramilitary covert action

More severe still are paramilitary (PM) covert actions, which involve the use of armed force overseas. Some examples include: the clandestine warfare waged by the CIA against communist guerrillas in Laos from 1962 to 1968 (an effort to protect U.S. troops in adjacent Vietnam); the unacknowledged sale of weapons abroad, as when the United States secretly sold missiles to Iran in the 1980s in exchange for its hoped-for influence over terrorists in Lebanon; the training, advising, and supplying of mercenaries to fight on behalf of America's foreign interests, such as the *contras* and the Afghan *mujahedeen*; and antiterrorist and security training for foreign intelligence services. However convenient for presidents as a means for avoiding the provisions of the War Powers Resolution and public debate about overt war-making, the paramilitary approach has been fraught with controversy. Critics recoil from Agency coups against foreign governments, arguing that covert action represents the ultimate perversion of America's democratic ideals – especially when the coup targets are democratically elected regimes. Others view the option as a useful instrument in the bag of foreign policy options, if necessary to help protect and advance the global interests of the United States.

Assassination plots

The CIA's schemes to kill individual enemies of the United States in foreign countries are a particularly controversial category of paramilitary activity. Over the years, the Agency developed a storehouse of lethal chemicals, along with several inventive delivery systems, for the purpose of assassination. The poisons, which included shellfish toxin ("saxitoxin") and cobra venom, were in enough supply and sufficiently deadly to elim-inate the entire population of a small city. One delivery system entailed first applying poison to a tiny dart the size of a sewing needle, labeled a "nondiscernible micro-bioinoculator" by an imaginative scientist in the Agency's DS&T. The needle was designed for firing by an electric dart gun, labeled a "noise-free disseminator" and resembling a .45 pistol with a short telescopic sight. The pistol could propel the dart silently toward the victim with an accuracy up to 250 feet – the ultimate murder weapon, able to kill without a sound or trace.

Murder high

The United States has resorted to assassination plots only infrequently and, at least with respect to foreign heads of state, never successfully – despite trying often in the case of Fidel Castro. In "Operation Mongoose," the Cuban president received during the 1960s the full attention of the CIA Operations Directorate: propaganda, political and economic action, and paramilitary operations. The Agency directed lethal drugs and poisons his way through various ingenious methods – over 30 times, according to former DCI Stansfield Turner. Among them: depilatory powder in his shoes, meant to enter Castro's bloodstream and make his charismatic beard fall off; LSD and botulinum toxin in his cigars, to dis-orient in the first instance and kill in the second; Madura-foot fungus in his underwater diving suit, causing a debilitating disease; and the poison Blackleaf-40, readied for injection into his skin through the fine tip of a DS&T-crafted ballpoint pen. These attempts all failed, because Castro was elusive and protected by a Soviet-trained corps of bodyguards in the KGB. So the Agency upped the ante. The DO mobilized organized crime figures who still had contacts in Cuba from pre-Castro days when Havana was a world gambling center. They sent assassins to Cuba. None succeeded.

As a way of sheltering the Eisenhower and Kennedy Administrations at the time from blame for the Agency's CIA assassination plots was a doctrine of decision-making known as "plausible deniability." Its purpose was to erase any traces of presidential involvement in the CIA's dirty work. Like Caesar's wife, the virtue and reputation of the United States had to be protected. If the Agency found it necessary to discuss an "extralegal" or questionable operation with a president, euphemisms and doubletalk were the order of the day. This would leave the nation's chief executive free to deny that the White House had granted specific authority for the Agency's mischief overseas. For covert actions – and especially assassination attempts – it was decision-making by a wink and a nod.

The controversy over assassination plots continues today. The second Bush Administration, and subsequently, Presidents Obama, Trump, and Biden have ordered the CIA to hunt down and kill identified members of terrorist organizations. The frequency of counterterrorism drone attacks has climbed sharply upward since first used by Bush II. In January of 2020, President Trump even went so far as to order the drone killing (this one carried out by the Defense Department) of an Iranian public figure, Qasem Soleimani. This rash act had the effect of inviting retribution against America's own public officials, a response that fortunately the Iranian government has not pursued, although it did carry out a counter-attack against U.S. troops stationed in Iraq, badly injuring several of them.

A further drone controversy: targeting errors occur from time to time and innocent civilians are periodically killed by mistake. In Pakistan, these tragedies have included a group of village elders meeting to discuss strategies for a more efficient mining of ore in the mountains. This "collateral damage," in the soulless Pentagon euphemism, has turned many Muslims against the United States who were otherwise pro-American.

Murder low

The most well-known operation to eliminate from the scene ("neutralize," in spy-speak) large numbers of lower-level foreign targets was the CIA's Phoenix program. The purpose of this program, carried out in South Vietnam as part of the American war effort in the 1960s and early 1970s, was to subdue the influence of the communists in the South Vietnamese countryside, especially the local Vietcong Infrastructure (VCI) allied with North Vietnam. According to former DCI William E. Colby, who for a time ran the program, some 20,000 VC leaders and sympathizers were killed as a result of its secret operations. He subsequently stressed that about 85 percent of those killed were engaged in military or paramilitary combat against South Vietnamese or American soldiers; and another 12 percent died at the hands of South Vietnamese security forces. Colby conceded, though, that assassinations might have taken place by over-zealous South Vietnamese, or even American, participants in the Phoenix program.

Covert action holds strong appeal, in light of the frustrations of diplomacy and the dangers – as well as the expense – of overt military conflict. In the global struggle with the Soviets during the Cold War, the United States had found an instrument of secret foreign policy that seemed to work splendidly, beginning in 1947, that is, until the disastrous invasion of Cuba at the Bay of Pigs in 1961.

Limits of covert action

The temptation to resort to secret power in foreign affairs has remained strong. "As you look ahead to the next ten or twenty years, we don't know when another kind of political crisis might arise in the world," DCI Colby argued, "and I think it is better that we have the ability to help people in these countries where that will happen, quietly and secretly, and not wait until we are faced with a military threat that has to be met by armed force." Other high-level witnesses appearing before the Congress also acknowledged the necessity of maintaining a covert action capability; but they have urged that this approach be adopted only in carefully restricted circumstances. "The guiding criterion," advised Clark Clifford, a former Secretary of Defense during the Johnson presidency and chief author of the National Security Act of 1947, "should be the test as to whether or not a certain covert project truly affects our national security." Cyrus Vance, who would soon become Secretary of State in the Carter Administration, similarly emphasized to a congressional committee his belief that "it should be the policy of the United States to engage in covert actions only when they are absolutely essential to the national security."

Arguably, some covert actions have been useful, as when the CIA helped the DoD in routing Al Qaeda and the Taliban regime in Afghanistan in the immediate wake of the 9/11 attacks against the United States; and the Agency's paramilitary activities against communists in Laos during the 1960s, who otherwise would have been fighting U.S. troops inside Vietnam. This approach to foreign policy, however, can also lead to the decline of constitutional government within the United States, as demonstrated by the attempts of NSC and CIA officials in the Reagan Administration to bypass the Congress in their conduct of the Iran-*contra* affair in the 1980s. In that controversial set of clandestine operations, the Reagan presidency and the CIA violated the law, including an existing arms embargo against Iran. Moreover, lawmakers had banned aid to the *contra* rebellion in Nicaragua, by way of the Boland Amendments sponsored by the House Permanent Select Committee on Intelligence (HPSCI), chaired by Edward P. Boland (D-Massachusetts). The Administration simply brushed aside the law – and the Constitution – as it bypassed the legislative appropriations process and raised money secretly for its clandestine operations from foreign countries and friendly former campaign contributors in the United States.

Covert action decision-making

With the passage of the Hughes-Ryan Act on December 30, 1974, the president had to approve – through a "finding" – all important covert actions, plus inform congressional oversight panels of these decisions. These two steps represented radical departures from earlier practice and tossed the doctrine of plausible denial into the dustbin. Moreover, with the Intelligence Oversight Act of 1980, the most important formal measure taken by the Congress to strengthen its control over intelligence operations, reformers took a firm stand in favor of prior (*ante facto*) notification on covert actions – not just after the fact (*ex post facto*), as the Hughes-Ryan statute had allowed. Regrettably, these rules were violated during the Iran-*contra* affair; but additional legislation has improved congressional supervision of covert actions, most notably the Intelligence Oversight Act of 1991, which further clarified and strengthened the guardrails for accountability over America's hidden foreign policy activities.

This intelligence oversight burden has become too onerous from the perspective of some intelligence professionals. "What we have is covert action by national consensus!" declared an Agency Deputy Director for Operations (DDO) in 1984. He believed that U.S. intelligence had become paralyzed, or at least maimed, by oppressive layers of decision-makers and overseers. Agency officers sometimes refer to strong accountability for covert action and other intelligence activities as "micromanagement" – too many executive and legislative policymakers with their clumsy fingers in the delicate wheels of America's spy machinery.

Intelligence reformers, though, point to the excessive discretionary authority allowed Agency operatives in the past, which led to the Bay of Pigs; the CIA's connections with the mob for murder plots against Castro; spying against U.S. antiwar protesters in the 1960s ("Operation CHAOS"); the use of covert action against foreign democratic governments (Chile, for instance); and the shocking Iran-*contra* scandal (among other examples). Representative Boland observed in the midst of that scandal that "the CIA was almost like a rogue elephant, doing what it wanted to do." Moreover, in defense of the new covert action review procedures, reformers stress that the process can move rapidly in times of emergency. Over secure telephones, approvals can be completed within hours when necessary. In normal times, though, there is time for debate by elected representatives of the American people in Congress, along with accountability, even within the heavily veiled side of America's government. Indeed, debate and accountability are the very anchors of democracy.

In recognition of the need for improved methods of covert action executive decision-making and congressional review in the wake of the Iran-*contra* affair, DCI William H. Webster (1987–1991) crafted a set of questions he posed inside the CIA that had to be answered satisfactorily before a covert action gained his backing:

- Is it legal (that is, in obeyance to the U.S. intelligence oversight statutes)?
- Is it consistent with American foreign policy and, if not, why not?
- Is it consistent with American values?
- If it became public, will it make sense to the American people?

This last standard is often referred to as the *New York Times* test.

The Webster decision criteria raised the bar for covert action approvals and moved the CIA more squarely into America's democratic framework of governance. Another former DCI, Robert M. Gates (1991–1993), has commented on the post-Iran-*contra* approach to intelligence supervision in the United States: "... some awfully crazy schemes would have been approved had everyone present not known and expected hard questions, debate, and criticism from the Hill. And when, on a few occasions, Congress was kept in the dark, and such schemes did proceed, it was nearly always to the lasting regret of the Presidents involved."

Notes

Valuable for understanding covert action are government reports issued by the Senate panel led by Frank Church: "Alleged Assassination Plots Involving Foreign Leaders," *Interim Report of the Senate Select Committee on Government Operations with Respect to Intelligence Activities*, U.S. Senate (November 20, 1975), as well as Anne Karalekas, "A History of Covert Action," Book IV, *Final Report*, U.S. Senate (April 23, 1976): 25–93. See, also, Malcolm Byrne, *Iran-Contra* (Lawrence: University Press of Kansas, 2014); William J. Daugherty, *Executive Secrets* (Lexington: University Press of Kentucky, 2004); Loch K. Johnson, *The Third Option* (New York: Oxford University Press, 2021); John Prados, *Presidents' Secret Wars* (New York: Morrow, 1969); and Gregory F. Treverton, *Covert Action* (New York: Basic Books, 1987). For the quotes in this chapter: "giving history a push," the author's interview with a DO official (February 11, 1986); "global challenge," Hugh Tovar in Roy Godson, ed., *Intelligence Requirements for the 1980s* (Washington, D.C.: National Strategy Information Center, 1981): 194–195; Grass and Church, respectively: *The Nation* (March 12, 1983): 30, and "Covert Action: Swampland of American Foreign Policy," *Bulletin of the Atomic Scientists* 32 (February 1976): 7–11; on assassinations, Church Committee *Report* (above), as well as Stansfield Turner, *Burn Before Reading* (New York: Hyperion, 2005): 98, and William E. Colby and Peter Forbath, *Honorable Men* (New York: Simon & Schuster, 1978): 272; Colby on covert action, "Gesprach mit William E. Colby," *Der Spiegel* 4 (January 23, 1978): 101; the Clifford and Vance testimony, Church Committee, *Hearings* (October 23, 1975); and Webster and Gates, Loch K. Johnson, *The Threat on the Horizon* (New York: Oxford University Press, 2010): 281, and Robert M. Gates, *From the Shadows* (New York: Simon & Schuster, 1996): 559. On the new era of accountability for covert action, see Loch K. Johnson, *Spy Watching* (New York: Oxford University Press, 2018).

13   Economic statecraft

With globalization has come intense competition for the United States in the international marketplace. Whether Americans are able to respond effectively to this commercial rivalry has become one of the great issues of foreign policy. In the final cabinet meeting of the Carter Administration, the president asked the departmental secretaries to reflect back on what each had learned during their time in office. Secretary of Defense Harold Brown replied: "I learned that if you don't have sustainable economics, you will not have a good defense. They go together. If we want to be strong, it begins with a good economy."

In 2020, the United States faced a harsh economic reality in world affairs. While America remained the largest economy in the world, comprising some 25 percent of all global output (far more than the next two countries, China and Japan, combined), the nation's trade deficit was some US$64 billion in July of that year, up 19 percent over the previous month – the largest monthly deficit since July 2008, in the middle of America's Great Recession. The imports of the United States rose to US$232 billion, an 11 percent increase, while exports climbed only slightly to US$168 billion. This cloud of economic distress that descended over the U.S. economy was, in large part, a result of job dislocations and the serious disruption of commercial ties caused worldwide by the COVID-19 pandemic. Like other countries, the United States was practically on a war footing, as it struggled to defeat the lethal and rapidly spreading virus, while trying to right the teetering economy the pandemic had brought in its wake.

Commerce as an instrument of American foreign policy

The setting in which international trade takes place has evolved in recent decades into a much more complex array of market relationships than was true immediately after the Second World War – the "globalization" defined earlier in this book as economic and other forms of increasing interdependence among nations. Today, a debt crisis in Greece can lead to a sudden panic on the New York Stock Exchange. A look at overall world trading patterns near the end of the Cold War reveals that most of these activities resided within the Western industrialized nations. Some 42 percent of the total world exports and imports took place within the circle of these democratic market economies; and over 50 percent of U.S. trade was with these nations.

America relies on imports most notably when it comes to passenger motor vehicles; trucks and buses; wearing apparel; iron and steel; consumer electronics; nonferrous metals; footwear; coffee, tea, and spices; natural gas; paper; telecommunications equipment; alcoholic beverages; toys and sporting goods; and fish. For some imports, the U.S. domestic economy provides no alternative products, as is the case presently for coffee and diamonds (for example). In the opposite direction, American exports consist chiefly of food products, chemicals, and machinery. The United States enjoys significant trade surpluses in some goods, including cereals and grains, aircraft equipment and spacecraft, oilseeds, computers, coal, scientific and engineering equipment, military arms and vehicles, construction equipment, plastic and rubber, cotton, animal feed, tobacco, power generating equipment, organic chemicals, and pharmaceutical products.

Among the various economic ties between the United States and the rest of the world, the most significant relationships are with China, Mexico, Canada, Japan, the United Kingdom, and Germany. The most noteworthy change in America's trading partners in recent years is the new high profile of China, with steadily rising economic transactions between the two major powers – at least until the Trump Administration began a trade war with the Chinese.

A rising China

China recently passed Japan as the world's second-largest economy after the United States. It is also the top-ranked trading nation in goods; the largest manufacturer; and the second-largest importer after America. During 2020, the first year of the pandemic (which originated in Wuhan, China), the Chinese economy grew at almost 5 percent, without monetizing debt, while all other major economies contracted. Given China's economic might and its growing military strength, the world had become bipolar again – as during the Cold War. This time, though, the superpowers are China and the United States, with the Russian economy only one-eighth the size of China's and its military spending just one-quarter its size. Japan and Germany lagged far behind China and the United States on the economic dimension of power, and, because of historical reasons, they had only modest military establishments.

The United States is China's foremost importer of goods and, indeed, trade in goods between the nations is almost US$2 billion *each day*. Nonetheless, some forecasters warn of an inevitable clash between America with its democratic principles but slow economic growth rate, on the one hand, and China with its illiberal political system and vibrant economy, on the other hand. By 2050, China is projected to have the world's largest economy, easing past the United States. Beyond profound philosophical differences about principles of government, several issues have troubled the U.S.-Chinese trading relationship. For one, America's current trade deficit with China has grown, as a result not only of the pandemic but also because of the ongoing trade war between the two nations initiated by President Trump.

Unlike the Soviet Union in the late 1940s under Stalin, with its expansionist moves into East Europe and Manchuria, the Chinese have fortunately displayed little outward aggression. Still, its communist leaders (like their counterparts in Russia) practice ruthless inward repression, including the gulag-like imprisonment of over a million Muslims – known as the Uighurs – in western China. The Chinese people suffer not only from a lack of political freedoms at home, but their homeland is surrounded by nations – Japan and Vietnam, for instance – who are wary and hostile toward them. Despite stunning economic growth rates that have pulled millions of Chinese from the depths of poverty and into middle-class status, this colossus of almost 1.5 billion people – the world's most populous nation – has deep-seated challenges at home. As John Cassidy observes, China is still a relatively poor country, with a per capita GDP of about $3,000 in 2008. By 2050, according to a recent study from the Carnegie Endowment, this figure will rise to about £33,000, which would still only place China roughly where Spain is today.

Economic competition between the United States and China will remain fierce. They need each other for trading purposes, though, and, as a result, the two nations are not necessarily on a collision course, bound for a new Cold War. While the current trade balance significantly favors China, economists discern undercurrents that will move the superpowers toward more of an equilibrium. Many U.S. products are avidly sought out by Chinese consumers. The Kentucky Fried Chicken franchise, for instance, is the most patronized fast-food chain in China. One of America's leading China experts, Professor David Shambaugh of George Washington University, recommends taking a page from the U.S.-Soviet periods of détente as a means for improving Sino-American relations, such as the pursuit of arms-control accords, the creation of better hotlines for communications between officials in Beijing and Washington, and engagement in regular military-to-military consultations.

Protectionism versus free trade

Negative trade statistics, plus the loss of sales for U.S. manufacturers overseas, traditionally cause a tide of protectionism to swell in company towns across America, that is, the support for the use of government tariffs and quotas against imports, as a means of protecting U.S. industries from foreign competition. Recent presidential candidates have successfully used protectionist appeals in Ohio and other primary states to garner votes from American workers in anguish over the decline of jobs and earning power. This was a top campaign priority for President Trump and, during his first three years in office, his Administration stimulated the creation of 6.6 million new jobs – a 4.4 percent increase over the Obama years (although President Obama was the one to initially stimulate this upward swing in job creation). Trump also sharply departed from America's traditional support in the modern era for open and free trade.

In contrast to these protectionist sentiments, President Reagan steadfastly defended a policy of free trade – the removal of government tariffs or other restrictions on international commercial transactions. Like his successors, though, Reagan applied behind-the-scenes pressure on the Japanese and other nations to buy more U.S. products.

President George H. W. Bush's North American Free Trade Agreement (NAFTA), a 1,100-page proposal to improve trading relations between the United States, Canada, and Mexico, became a source of controversy. Bush argued in favor of the pact in 1991 on grounds that "a NAFTA offers an historic opportunity to bring together the energies and talents of three great nations ... [and to] create jobs and promote growth in the United States." Yet many Americans, labor unions not the least, feared that U.S. companies – jobs – might move south of the border in search of cheap labor. Others warned that Mexico would fail to uphold America's strong environmental standards, or its laws regulating labor standards and worker rights. Presidents Clinton and Trump both renegotiated the NAFTA during their presidencies, gaining improvements for American workers. The judgment on NAFTA remains mixed but, on balance, most economists are favorably disposed toward this Western Hemisphere common market.

Improving market competitiveness

The United States has lost some competitive advantages in world trade, but improvements are possible. American business personnel could become, for instance, more proficient in the study of the product distribution system in China and Japan, and could devote more time to learning the languages of these important nations. In Manhattan, hundreds of Chinese and Japanese businesspeople can be found negotiating deals in perfectly acceptable English, while probably less than a hundred of their American counterparts are similarly engaged in Beijing or Tokyo speaking the native tongues. The competitive edge of the United States for high-technology products has also eroded. While America remains the chief exporter of high-tech products, the advanced industrialized nations are rapidly closing the gap. Over 40 percent of the college graduates in Japan and West Germany are in engineering and the sciences, compared with some 16 percent in the United States. That America came in 23rd or 24th in most subjects during a recent international education test, including average math scores that put U.S. students below 30 other countries, is further troubling news that augurs poorly for America's future global competitiveness.

The multinationals

The international economic system is made all the more complicated by the existence of multinational corporations (MNCs), which have foreign subsidiaries that extend the production and marketing of these firms beyond the borders of any one country. Some observers view these corporations positively as benign contributors to world trade; others see them as the spearhead of imperialism. Most political economists, though, look on the MNC as an inevitable outcome of globalization, with some good and some bad effects. In market economies like Canada, France, and Great Britain, for instance, American-owned MNCs seem to have produced positive results in the host economy, especially in capital formation and improved access to advanced technology and management skills. Yet the MNCs have also cast a long shadow. Some have displayed alarming predatory behavior, exemplified by the efforts of the International Telephone and Telegraph Company (ITT) to undermine the freely-elected government of Chile under President Allende in the 1970s.

Trade sanctions

Trade sanctions can be significant tools of foreign policy. In hopes of halting Iran's production of nuclear weapons, for example, the United States has ratcheted up its efforts to coordinate global trade sanctions against Tehran. The Obama Administration claimed in 2011 that U.S. trade sanctions had left the Iranian regime economically strained, diplomatically isolated, and torn by internal divisions; and the Trump Administration turned the screws even tighter on Iran. By all accounts, though, the government in Tehran continued its development of a nuclear weapons program. A chief goal of the United States is to use smart sanctions, that is, economic inducements that punish the elites in a target country, but not the average person on the street. The United States drew back from its talk of cutting off refined gasoline products to Iran in 2010, out of concern that this approach would hurt the masses more than the government in Tehran.

The adoption of other economic carrots and sticks against a recalcitrant nation (including boycotts and embargoes) often fails, because other nations refused to honor these restrictions. When the United States sought to deprive the Soviet Union of grain during the Cold War, for instance, Canada and Argentina were pleased to fill the demand. More recently, Iran has skirted U.S. sanctions simply by exporting more of its oil to China. Further, some countries are able to resist outside pressures, regardless of internal economic deprivations. Despite a sharp international reaction that included threats of economic reprisal against the regime's brutality, Chinese leaders remained adamant about snuffing out all vestiges of revolutionary fervor among their young people in 1989, executing several leaders of a pro-democracy movement.

Foreign aid

Foreign aid may be defined as economic and military assistance on a government-to-government level, or through government-supported agencies or programs. Israel has been the largest cumulative beneficiary of America's foreign assistance program since the Second World War, until recently displaced (temporarily) by U.S. efforts to help stabilize the pro-Western government in Afghanistan, which was under siege by Taliban fighters. According to State Department data, the top recipients of American foreign aid in 2009 were (in annual figures):

Afghanistan: US$2.66 billion	West Bank and Gaza: US$0.97 billion
Israel: US$2.55 billion	Jordan: US$0.72 billion
Egypt: US$1.44 billion	Iraq: US$0.61 billion
Pakistan: US$1.44 billion	Ethiopia: US$0.54 billion

While these are large sums of money, foreign aid has accounted for only about 1 percent of the U.S. budget in recent years. "The total cost in tax dollars for all our security and economic assistance programs in the developing countries is $43.91 per person," reported Secretary of State George P. Shultz during the Reagan Administration. "In contrast," he continued, "we Americans spend $104 per person a year for TV and radio sets, $35 per person per year for barbershop and beauty parlors, $97 per person per year for soap and cleaning supplies, and $21 per person per year for flowers and potted plants." In the 1970s, the Paris-based Organisation for Economic Co-operation and Development (OECD) proposed a foreign aid standard for the wealthy nations of at least 0.7 percent of their gross national income (GNI). Using this index, America ranked next to last among the industrialized nations as an aid-giver in 1987 (at 0.2 percent, above only Austria's 0.17 percent). By 2007, Austria had improved its standing, while the United States moved to the end of the line with a 0.16 percentage score. Only Denmark, Luxembourg, the Netherlands, Norway, and Sweden met the OECD target in 2008. Such comparisons, though, fail to take into account America's generous outpouring of private monies sent abroad for humanitarian purposes. Alex Perry, a journalist with *Time* magazine, estimates that private foreign aid from Americans reached US$37.3 billion in 2008 – more than US$10 billion over the U.S. government's aid programs that year.

The disparity in lifestyles between the rich and poor nations has created strong resentment in the developing nations among those living on US$1–2 a day (or less in some places). Economist Robert L. Heilbroner has compared the world to "an immense train, in which a few passengers, mainly in the advanced capitalist world, ride in first-class coaches, in conditions of comfort unimaginable to the enormously greater numbers jammed into the cattle cars that make up the bulk of the train's carriages." The Kennedy Administration established two successful programs to help address these conditions abroad: the Peace Corps and the Alliance for Progress, the latter designed to strengthen the U.S. economic aid package for Latin America. In 2020, the Peace Corps had 7,6367 volunteers serving in 61 nations around the world, with 45 percent in Africa and 19 percent in Latin America –the two largest contingents.

By the mid-1970s, however, pessimism about the usefulness of foreign aid had spread throughout Washington, D.C. Aid had long had its critics – "the greatest give-away in history," perennially groused Representative

Otto Passman (D-Louisiana), the powerful chairman of the House Appropriations Subcommittee on Foreign Assistance – but opposition on Capitol Hill toward foreign assistance has become more extensive. Despite the billions of dollars worth of U.S. assistance pumped into Vietnam in the late 1960s and early 1970s, the failure to achieve success in that part of the world cast a pall over the notion of foreign aid programs. Important, too, in the demise of support for foreign assistance was the lingering doubt in Washington that the aid actually had much of an effect on a poor nation's development. "We don't know how to use aid to reduce poverty," wrote prominent journalist David Brooks. He pointed to China, which has received little foreign aid but has experienced significant declines in poverty, while just the opposite is true for Haiti.

Was foreign aid worth the cost, critics asked, especially when the United States has underdeveloped areas of its own where the limited resources of the taxpayer might be spent? "I go home and see farmers' wives cry in front of me," said one Midwest lawmaker, who also happened to be chairman of the Appropriations Subcommittee on Foreign Operations, the key House panel on foreign assistance. "Don't tell me about the Philippines."

What have been the results of America's investment in foreign aid over the years? One scholarly review could only answer: "The impact of foreign aid remains obscure and perplexing." During the 1980s, the Congress began to routinely slash aid for some nations by over 50 percent. Only those countries with effective lobbies in Washington – most notably, Israel – managed to dodge the axe. In 2011, deep spending reductions came in food and medicine for Africa; in disaster relief for Pakistan and Japan; in political and economic assistance for new democracies in the Middle East; and in support for the Peace Corps. Only Israel escaped the funding reductions.

Given America's financial stresses at home since the recession of 2008, now exacerbated by the COVID-19 pandemic, some budget cutting was to be expected in the aid program. Yet on moral grounds alone, to what extent can the United States afford to turn a cold shoulder to the needs of developing regions of the world? Besides, some aid programs have produced dramatic successes. For instance, in Sauri, Kenya, a U.S. government project spearheaded by Columbia University economist Jeffrey D. Sachs has led to the doubling of agricultural yields; a drop in child mortality rates of 30 percent; soaring school attendance; an increase in the use of bed nets against mosquito-carrying malaria; and widespread cellphone ownership (a sign of prosperity in rural Africa). Professor Sachs places an emphasis on tightly focused, technology-based programs that proceed across a broad front simultaneously, including health care, education, and job training. The challenge is how to move from his focus on small villages to apply these methods successfully to larger areas and populations in Africa and elsewhere.

Important, too, is a more scientific approach to measuring the effects of various foreign aid programs. Economist Esther Duflo and her colleagues at MIT are engaged in research on these effects by using laboratory methods, such as control groups and evidence-based experiments, to test the value of aid initiatives. In one experiment, for example, researchers found that the usage rates of malaria-fighting mosquito bed nets are the same, whether African villagers pay for them or get them free; but that they are more likely to buy them in the future if they are given them for free or pay only a little at first. Hard data of this kind hold promise for improvements in the delivery of America's aid programs.

Notes

On U.S. global economic challenges, see David A. Baldwin, *Economic Statecraft* (Princeton, NJ: Princeton University Press, 1985); I. M. Destler, *American Trade Politics: System Under Stress*, 3rd ed. (Washington, D.C.: Institute for International Economics, 1995); Robert Gilpin, *The Challenge of Global Capitalism: The World Economy in the 21st Century* (Princeton, NJ: Princeton University Press, 2000); Robert L. Heilbroner, *An Inquiry into the Human Prospect* (New York: Norton, 1975); C. Donald Johnson, *The Wealth of a Nation: A History of Trade Politics in America* (New York: Oxford University Press, 2018); Meghan O'Sullivan, *Shrewd Sanctions* (Washington, D.C.: Brookings Institution Press, 2003); Jeffrey D. Sachs, *The End of Poverty: Economic Possibilities for Our Time* (New York: Penguin, 2005); and Joseph E. Stiglitz and Andrew Charlton, *Fair Trade for All* (New York: Oxford University Press, 2005). For quotes and related references in this chapter, see: on Brown, Walter F. Mondale, *The Good Fight* (New York: Scribner's, 2010): 284–285; on China, John Cassidy, "Enter the Dragon," *The New Yorker* (December 13, 2010): 14, and on its 5 percent growth during 2019, investor Ray Dalio, quoted in

The New York Times (November 1, 2020): SR. Professor Shambaugh's suggestions are cited by Nicholas Kristof, "Biden's Nightmare May be China," *The New York Times* (January 31, 2021): SR9. On Warren, see Georgetown University Professor Charles A. Kupchan, *The Washington Post* (November 24, 2020); on Shultz, Bernard Gwertzman, "A Citizen Pays $34 for Aid," *The New York Times* (February 25, 1983): A1; Alex Perry, *Lifeblood* (New York: PublicAffairs, 2011); Robert L. Heilbroner, *An Inquiry into the Human Prospect* (New York: Norton, 1975): 39; Passman, quoted in Ian J. Bickerton, "Foreign Aid," in Alexander DeConde, ed., *Encyclopedia of American Foreign Policy*, Vol. II (New York: Scribner's, 1978): 375; David Brooks, "The Underlying Tragedy," *The New York Times* (January 15, 2010): 21; Midwest lawmaker, quoted by Peter Osterlund, "Congress Tightens Foreign-Aid Screws," *Christian Science Monitor* (September 18, 1986): A1; Carl Rowan, "American Ignorance," *Atlanta Constitution* (November 4, 1979): 14; on Sachs, see Jeffrey Gettleman, "Shower of Aid Brings Flood of Progress," *The New York Times* (March 9, 2010): A9; and Esther Duflo, "Marshaling the Evidence," *RAND Review* (Spring 2010): 9.

In 2004, photographs obtained by the media revealed that U.S. military intelligence personnel had engaged in harsh interrogation measures against prisoners in Iraq. The victims were men of all ages, captured after America's invasion of Iraq in 2003 and held in a Baghdad prison known as Abu Ghraib [pronounced "á boo gráb"]. Several of the prisoners were blindfolded and stripped before snarling police dogs and women interrogators. Some had to stand, hooded, on boxes with electrical wires running to sensitive body parts; some died from the rough handling. Other reports surfaced in American newspapers about U.S. intelligence officers using waterboarding techniques against Iraqi detainees and suspected Qaeda terrorists. With waterboarding, a victim is tied down on his back, and his face is covered with a cloth; then a steady stream of water is poured on the face, producing a sensation of drowning. Several high-level officials in the second Bush Administration, including Vice President Dick Cheney, publicly denied that this method amounted to torture, even though at the end of the Second World War the United States prosecuted Japanese soldiers as war criminals for waterboarding American GIs. Eventually, the Bush White House abandoned the technique, and the incoming Obama Administration publicly acknowledged that waterboarding was torture and banned its use.

The importance of ethical and cultural values

The nightmares that emerged from Abu Ghraib were soon joined by other disturbing revelations. In Guantánamo, American military personnel held additional detainees from the war in Iraq, or men captured in Afghanistan as a result of the CIA sweep across that country in 2001 in search of Qaeda members. Charges were never brought against these prisoners; they languished in their cells without legal counsel. Newspaper stories emerged, too, about secret CIA prisons in Eastern Europe – "black sites" – where yet more detainees had been sequestered. Further, documented reports surfaced about the CIA's involvement in extraordinary rendition, whereby Agency personnel kidnapped suspected terrorists off the streets of Stockholm or some other European or Middle Eastern location, then, for purposes of interrogation, flew them to Egypt or other nations less squeamish than the United States about human rights abuses. At these interrogation sites, foreign intelligence officers would torture the suspects and forward the information to the CIA or U.S. military intelligence agencies. This arrangement supposedly left Washington officials with an opportunity to claim plausible denial, as if it were so easy for them to escape culpability for these unsavory interrogation methods.

As legal scholars Cole and Dempsey have noted with respect to Abu Ghraib, this departure from America's long-standing principles against torture and other mistreatments of prisoners was "not only wrong but actually harms national security by fueling anti-American sentiment." The United States was entitled to hunt down the 9/11 attackers, of course, using the full array of overt and covert operations in Afghanistan (where Al Qaeda maintained a haven). In retaliation against the 9/11 attacks, however, critics maintain that the second Bush Administration had adopted excessive measures and tarnished America's most important possession: the nation's good name and high moral standing in the world.

Ethical considerations have long been a part of U.S. foreign policy, as illustrated by the missionary zeal at the end of the nineteenth century that sent thousands of Americans overseas to disseminate religious moral teachings; and by President Wilson's call for transparency in global diplomacy ("open covenants openly arrived at"), as well as the revulsion over CIA assassination plots that led to an executive order in 1976 signed by President Gerald R. Ford banning this approach to foreign policy (except in times of authorized war). Journalist Bob Woodward has expressed a view held by many Americans regarding the moral blindfolds worn by the DCI in the Reagan Administration, William J. Casey, an instigator of the Iran-*contra* scandal. "If there's a tragic part of Casey, and I guess there is, it is that he ultimately didn't realize what this country is about," Woodward wrote. "That we are different ... that we can't go out and try to get the Saudi intelligence service to kill people we don't like, because in America we don't do that in secret, because that tells the world who we are. It tells *us* who we are."

Ethical dilemmas in foreign policy

Whether to use a nuclear weapon against the Japanese in 1945 was a decision laden with painful ethical implications. The atomic bomb had the destructive power to level cities in seconds, sending civilian populations – noncombatant women, children, and the aged among them – to a fiery death. Even those who survived might wish they had been at ground zero, because of the long-range illnesses and even genetic alterations that can accompany exposure to radioactive emissions from a nuclear bomb. Still, as in so many foreign policy decisions, a failure to use the bomb would have had ethical implications, too. Every week during the war in the Pacific, hundreds of American soldiers paid Nature's debt. The United States lost 75,000 soldiers on the island of Okinawa alone. By April 1945, kamikaze raids had sent to the bottom of the Pacific Ocean 34 U.S. ships, including three aircraft carriers. An invasion of Japan would probably have incurred, according to estimates by the joint chiefs of staff at the time, several hundred thousand American casualties, as well as an even larger number of Japanese deaths – far more loss of life than what one atomic bomb, or even two, would produce. Primarily to save as many American lives as possible, President Truman made the decision to use the ultimate weapon against Japan.

America's use of atomic weapons

The decision was not made lightly. Truman, Secretary of War Henry L. Stimson, and others high in the Administration agonized over the dreadful power of the new weapon. Even after Truman arrived at the decision to use the atomic bomb, Stimson argued on moral grounds against certain targets. The government's target-selection committee had identified Kyoto, the former capital of Japan – a city of great beauty and cultural significance – as one potential target. That city was spared, however, after Stimson informed Truman in a revealing mixture of realism and idealism that "Japan's help against Russia might be needed in the future but that if Americans destroyed this cultural shrine they would never be forgiven."

Some critics question whether the use of an atomic bomb against any Japanese city was necessary. They suggest that U.S. authorities could have told their Japanese counterparts about the weapon, followed by a demonstration of its effects on an uninhabited Pacific atoll near Japan, or perhaps dropped the bomb on a flotilla of Japanese naval ships at sea. The rebuttal to these arguments is twofold. First, the United States only had a couple of atomic bombs and could ill-afford to use one in a demonstration that might have been a dud – and a windfall for Japanese scientists to capture and dissect. Second, the Japanese were so resolute in their determination to fight down to the last soldier, in fidelity to the ancient samurai code of the Japanese warrior class, that the Truman Administration estimated it would take something as profoundly shocking as the nuclear bombing of a major city to convince them that further resistance was futile. Critics of the bombing maintain, also, that the United States should have at least provided a clear warning to the Japanese about which city was targeted, so noncombatants could have been evacuated. Yet a warning might have caused the Japanese to gather American prisoners of war into the target city as a means for deterring the bombing. Further, the Japanese might have alerted their meager air defenses to the impending attack, concentrating their efforts around the target city.

Even more controversial than the bombing of Hiroshima was the attack only three days later against Nagasaki. This brief interval left little time for the Japanese war cabinet to assemble, consider the dangers of further delay, and arrive at a declaration of surrender. The U.S. military advanced the timetable for the bombing of Nagasaki by a few days because of approaching bad weather. Critics maintain that this was hardly a satisfactory reason for extinguishing the lives of 40,000 people when a second bomb might have proved unnecessary.

Nuclear deterrence

Nothing so defines the era that followed the Second World War as the existence of nuclear weapons. Their proliferation and stockpiling have led not only to a widespread sense of anxiety in the world about their possible detonation again, but have also raised subtle yet profound ethical questions about nuclear warfare and how to guard against it. One school of thought argues that America's reliance on nuclear weapons during the Cold War to keep the superpowers at bay (the theory of deterrence) must now be rejected, for it is patently wrong to place in jeopardy the lives of millions of noncombatant civilians. This argument represents a radical critique of current policy. In its stress on the wrongness of even the *threat* to kill – the very core of deterrence – this critique is in harmony with the beliefs of the German philosopher Immanuel Kant (1724–1804). "Do what is right though the world should perish," he admonished. Above all else, he cherished the moral purity of the individual.

Applying the logic of this argument to nuclear deterrence, modern-day Kantians insist that what one ethically cannot do – murder millions of innocent men, women, and children – one cannot *intend* to do either, with nuclear missiles ready for firing at a moment's notice. Therefore, the nuclear option must be discarded altogether. In this spirit, the theologian Paul Ramsey draws an analogy between nuclear deterrence and the tying of babies to the bumpers of automobiles during the holiday season. Under these conditions, people would presumably drive more carefully and lives would be saved – a moral good. The method used, however, would be so repugnant as to be clearly wrong and unacceptable.

A second school in Western moral tradition, that of the consequentialists, offers a different perspective – one that highlights the outcome of an act, not the goal of maintaining the goodness of the individual involved. From this vantage point, nuclear deterrence serves a useful purpose, despite the sword of Damocles that it suspends above humanity. Since the bombing of Nagasaki, no nuclear weapon has been fired in anger; the world has escaped the outbreak of global conflict between major powers, a third world war, perhaps in part as a consequence of the deterrent effect provided by these weapons. The existence of nuclear weapons aimed at one another has become a part of the human condition ("existential deterrence"), to be accepted as the price one must pay to keep a balance of power and, thereby, thwart aggression by the major nations. For con-sequentialists, the *effect* of one's decision is of overriding importance, not the moral purity of the individual decision-maker.

Intelligence

Sometimes America's intelligence agencies have recruited individuals of notably dubious character, including former Nazis after the Second World War, to spy on behalf of the United States. In 1995, during the Clinton Administration, DCI John Deutch issued new regulations to prevent the recruitment of particularly despicable assets abroad. These regulations became known as the "Deutch rules." The stimulus was the case of a Colonel Alpirez in Guatemala, accused of complicity in the murder of a U.S. citizen at the same time the Colonel was also on the CIA payroll. Deutch expressed concern that the Agency had failed to keep Congress and the Justice Department properly informed about developments in this situation, as required by law. In the light of the Alpirez case, Deutch informed lawmakers that he intended to issue additional restrictive guidelines to Agency field officers "that offer clear guidance on this subject beyond previous directives." It would take time to change the "culture or mind-set" at Langley, he cautioned senators, perhaps requiring years "not weeks or months."

Deutch informed reporters that his guidelines would require CIA officers to become more discriminating in their recruitment of spies. He was aware, he said, that "... you are not going to be able to do the clandestine collection of intelligence with all wonderful and nice people." Nevertheless, the Agency would have to "balance here the character of the individual with respect to the intelligence you are gathering." These rules would stamp the DCI, at least for some critics (especially in the CIA's Operations Directorate), as hopelessly naive about the sordid reality of what it takes to gather humint. As a senior intelligence officer told a Presidential Commission in 1995: "It may be necessary to recruit criminals and crooks; you can't rely on the local minister for espionage." Another intelligence officer ridiculed the "motherhood and apple pie intelligence" advocated by Deutch.

Human rights

A display at the Carter Presidential Library in Atlanta proudly proclaims that "no issue was closer to Jimmy Carter than human rights." A deeply religious, born-again Christian, President Carter blended his foreign policy with a larger measure of moralism than any other president since Woodrow Wilson. Carter's dedication to human rights focused on the dignity of human beings around the world, including the fundamental right to freedom from repression. The President's national security adviser, Dr. Zbigniew Brzezinski, chastised Henry Kissinger for a "tendency to dismiss moral concerns in foreign policy as somehow equivalent to sentimentality." Carter's second Secretary of State, former Senator Edmund S. Muskie (D-Maine) added: "We stand for the right of people to be free of torture and repression, to choose their leaders, to participate in the decisions that affect their daily lives, to speak and write and travel freely." In Muskie's view, military arms were insufficient to defend America's vital interests: "We must also arm ourselves with the conviction that our values have increasing power in today's world." Understanding the limitations of pursuing human rights as a foreign policy objective, the Carter Administration adopted what Muskie referred to as a "practical approach" – doing what it could, where it could, "holding up the banner of human rights."

Quality of life

Just as disconcerting to observers as political repression throughout the world are the terrible conditions under which citizens born into poor countries must live. In Haiti, the average income per person is less than US$1 a day, one in five children dies before age five, and only 20 percent of the people have access to clean drinking water. Such statistics are all too common around the globe. Alarming, too, and raising additional ethical issues, is the damage being done to the world's environment by the growth-oriented industrialized societies. Noting the stress evident already in each of the earth's major biological systems – oceanic fisheries, grasslands, forests, and crop lands – an authority on global ecology argues that "if civilization as we know it is to survive, [an] ethic of accommodation must replace the prevailing growth ethic." Standing next to the basic human rights of freedom and dignity, of basic nourishment and shelter, is this ethics of ecology.

Charting a moral course

Moral questions are an inescapable part of American foreign policy. Since the world continues to be dominated by calculations of military strength, the perspective of the realist with its emphasis on the balancing of military power will no doubt remain the core consideration in the minds of policymakers, at least for the foreseeable future. After all, the failure of military balance can produce decidedly immoral results, as humanity has learned from two world wars. The failure of the League of Nations and the naivety of Neville Chamberlain eroded the world's faith in idealism as an approach to foreign policy. Yet who would be so bold as to deny that the power of principle – the pursuit of high ideals – can hold strong sway over the opinions of human beings around the world? "Should we use military power to intimidate smaller nations? Should we no longer stand up for the ideals we believe and that we share with all humanity?" asked Vice President Walter Mondale in 1980. "I reject that view as naive and dangerous," he answered, adding that "strength without principle is weakness." At Texas A&M University on the eve of his retirement in December of 1992, President George H. W. Bush reminded his audience that "our country's tradition of idealism [has made us] unique among nations."

The influences of America's moral standing and cultural values, what Professor Joseph S. Nye has referred to as "soft power," are a vital part of U.S. foreign policy. America's grand strategy in world affairs will have to continue the search for a proper blend of hard power (the instruments of the military and economic statecraft) and soft power (the attractive quality of U.S. democratic values). In Nye's phrase, "smart power." A contemporary Chinese scholar, Yan Xuetong, predicts that his country will win the race with the United States for world leadership. "It is the battle for people's hearts and minds that will determine who eventually prevails," he writes. "And, as China's ancient philosophers predicted, the country that displays more humane authority will win." One cannot quarrel with his criterion for success. The world will be watching to see which superpower displays more "humane authority" in the coming years.

Notes

For thoughtful studies into questions of ethical and cultural considerations in foreign policy, see: Lester R. Brown, *The Twenty-Ninth Day: Accommodating Human Needs and Numbers to the Earth's Resources* (New York: Norton, 1978); Joseph S. Nye Jr., *Ethics and Foreign Policy: An Occasional Paper* (Wye Plantation, MD: Aspen Institute for Humanistic Studies, 1985), as well as *Nuclear Ethics* (New York: Free Press, 1986) and *Soft Power: The Means to Success in World Politics* (New York: PublicAffairs, 2009); James P. Pfiffner, *Torture as Public Policy: Restoring U.S. Credibility on the World Stage* (Boulder, CO: Paradigm, 2010); Samantha Powers, *"A Problem From Hell": American and the Age of Genocide* (New York: Basic Books, 2002); Kenneth W. Thompson,

Morality and Foreign Policy (Baton Rouge: Louisiana State University, 1980); and Andrew Vincent, *The Politics of Human Rights* (New York: Oxford University Press, 2010). For quotes in this chapter, see David Cole and James X. Dempsey, *Terrorism and the Constitution* (New York: Free Press, 2006): x–xi; Woodward, remarks, "Secret Intelligence," PBS (February 13, 1989); Deutch rules, James Risen, "CIA to Issue Guidelines on Hiring Foreign Operatives," *The New York Times* (June 30, 1995): A4; on "crooks" and "motherhood," Loch K. Johnson, *The Threat on the Horizon* (New York: Oxford University Press, 2011): 249; on Brzezinski and Muskie, respectively, remarks, Platform Committee, Democratic National Committee, Washington, D.C. (June 12, 1980), and Muskie's "Human Freedom," *Current Policy No. 208*, U.S. Department of State (August 7, 1980): 3; and Joseph S. Nye Jr, *The Power to Lead* (New York: Oxford University Press, 2008): x.

PART V

The challenges ahead

15 A new American foreign policy

The prominence of the United States as a world power is a relatively new phenomenon. As George F. Kennan recalls, at the beginning of the twentieth century America's foreign policy was guided by "the concepts and methods of a small neutral nation." When he began his distinguished diplomatic career in the 1920s, the Department of State was (as he notes in his memoirs) "a quaint old place, with its law-office atmosphere, its cool dark corridors, its swinging doors, its brass cuspidors, its black leather rocking chairs, and the grandfather's clock in the Secretary of State's office." Those simple days are gone. The Department of State is now a sprawling building with seemingly endless hallways, government-gray desks, intricate operating procedures, and thousands of harried officials – in short, a modern bureaucracy.

The life of the Foreign Service officer overseas has changed dramatically, too. Seldom in earlier times were the lives of American diplomats at risk. The 73 who died in the first 189 years of the nation's history were, in almost all cases, the victims of shipwrecks, natural disasters, or tropical diseases. Since 1965, however, more than 80 have died at the hands of terrorists, including seven ambassadors in the past 16 years. In place of the once attractive prospect of living abroad, with inexpensive housing and affordable servants, villas with tennis courts and swimming pools, frond-trimmed verandas with lazy fans and trays of tax-free Scotch, today's diplomat faces the constant threat of harassment and terror.

Just as distant countries have grown more dangerous to Americans, so have they become more important. As Americans learned tragically in 2001, the world is increasingly difficult to ignore with its potential for terrorist attacks; the spread of sophisticated weaponry; the trading opportunities, and barriers, that affect the vitality of America's domestic economy; the need for access to global mineral resources vital to industrial manufacturing; the vanishing rainforests with their precious flora and fauna that help keep nature's balance; the human rights abuses wrought by corrupt dictators. The early American colonists also faced enormous challenges, surrounded as they were on one side by an ocean dominated by powerful, hostile navies and on the other side by a vast wilderness; nonetheless, the contemporary perils of terrorism and WMD, as well as the world's intricate patterns of trade interdependence, sudden pandemics, and a rising level of environmental pollution, have made this age one of much greater complexity and risk.

At the same time, advances in knowledge from medicine and astrophysics to communications and the art of governing encourage the hope that human beings are becoming better equipped to cope with the challenges before us – although this latter proposition has been sorely tested by the spectacle on January 6, 2021, of right-wing mobs storming the U.S. Capitol in an attack against democracy. Other shadows darken optimistic forecasts. As the twenty-first century unfolds, Americans face four major foreign policy weaknesses that must be overcome if this nation wishes to remain a leading world power. The first is the parochialism of U.S. citizens; the second, a disarray within the institutions of American government that plan and implement foreign policy; the third, the nation's habit of turning to war-fighting, instead of advancing U.S. interests through less extreme means; and, fourth, a tendency of Americans to intervene in the affairs of other countries.

Citizen awareness of global affairs

One of the most discouraging shortcomings in global leadership, and one each citizen can do something about, is the inadequate preparation of Americans to assume positions of responsibility in Washington's foreign policy institutions. Or, for that matter, even as voters to evaluate the foreign policy arguments made by candidates for high office. Consider the results from surveys on citizen awareness in the United States about world geography – one telling index of a citizen's interest in, and understanding of, international relations. A few months before the United States led a multinational invasion force into Iraq in 2003, a National Geographic Society survey found that only about one in seven

(13 percent) of Americans between the ages of 18 and 24 could find Iraq, Iran, or Israel on a world map. Only 17 percent could locate Afghanistan, where the United States was already at war. Overall, Americans came in next to last in the quiz, above Mexico, with a "D" grade. America's citizens will remain unable to appraise the foreign policy decisions of their public officials unless and until they learn more about the geography, culture, languages, and politics of other lands. Nor can this nation comfortably wear the mantle of world leadership if its citizens express ignorance of, and little interest in, world affairs.

Overcoming institutional and political polarization

A further challenge is for Washington officials to work with one another more effectively, in a spirit of comity that spreads across the executive, legislative, and judicial branches of government, engendering a mutual respect for the involvement of each branch in the making of foreign policy. Intolerable in a democracy are executive subterfuges epitomized by President Lyndon Johnson's hidden escalation of the war in Vietnam or, needless to say, the attempt by President Trump to incite a coup against Congress in the waning days of his presidency.

Institutional tensions will continue to interrupt the smooth functioning of the government from time to time, even under the best of circumstances when both the executive and legislative branches are trying to act in good faith and with a spirit of cooperation. The nation's founders, after all, explicitly sought to build into the Constitution checks on the misuse of power, and this arrangement is bound to lead to institutional friction. The appropriate remedy in a democracy when governing institutions are at loggerheads over major policy initiatives is open debate before the court of public opinion, followed by efforts to compromise divergent views, then a majority vote up or down in the Congress on a proposal – with 51 votes the victory benchmark, not the 60-vote rule of recent years, which practically guarantees paralysis on Capitol Hill.

This is the framework laid out by the Constitution, not the practices too often seen in recent decades of lying to congressional committees; ignoring statutory reporting requirements; engaging in endless filibusters on practically every major bill; dirt road politics that concentrates more on scoring rhetorical points against the opposition party than working together toward solving the nation's problems with bipartisan creativity; and ignoring legal restrictions on foreign operations, such as occurred during the Iran-*contra* scandal. Partisan polarization is another sobering challenge to democracy. The acrimony that arose between the Democratic and Republican parties during the Reagan era "confused our allies and emboldened our enemies," remembers Senator David Boren (D-Oklahoma), chair of his chamber's Intelligence Committee. Partisan vitriol has further intensified and threatens to cripple the ability to govern the United States.

Toward greater international empathy

Another disquieting weakness of America's foreign policy has been the tendency to exaggerate military threats abroad, then to respond with the war-making power. You "cannot relax for a minute," the Reagan Administration's Secretary of Defense, Caspar W. Weinberger, warned about possible Soviet aggression. Troops to Lebanon, the farcical Grenada operation, the "secret" war in Nicaragua, an American armada in the Persian Gulf without strategy or timetable – during the Reagan years practically every U.S. intervention abroad became justified as part of an anti-Soviet crusade.

Similarly, since the 9/11 attacks, Washington has allowed the fear of terrorism to draw the United States into two major wars in the highly inhospitable locations of Iraq and Afghanistan. In fact, though, Al Qaeda is a small sect – in 2010, an estimated 50 men in Afghanistan and some 300 in Pakistan and, today, not much larger. Many counterterrorism experts believe that *jihadists* are best captured or killed by small-scale interventions using CIA paramilitary operatives and special forces operating in tandem with local pro-West armies.

One of the major challenges faced by nations during the Cold War and today is, as former President Jimmy Carter has written, "the increasing disharmony and lack of understanding between rich and poor nations." In a 2010 commencement address at George Washington University,

Michelle Obama, the wife of President Obama, suggested an alternative way to make use of America's time and money. "Imagine a community whose first experience with America is a group of youth on winter break standing side by side with them building homes," she said in her commencement speech. "Imagine a country shattered by a catastrophic earthquake when they see wave after wave of rescuers and doctors and relief workers all wearing the Stars and Stripes on their sleeve. Imagine how powerful that is. Imagine what impact thousands of stories like that today can have a decade from now." One such story should be an energetic effort by the United States to help other nations develop anti-COVID vaccines for their citizens.

An end to compulsive interventionism

Fixated on the Soviet Union during the Cold War, the United States abandoned its traditional instincts of caution in foreign affairs and instead pursued a policy of compulsive interventionism. Leaders like Secretary of State John Foster Dulles during the Eisenhower Administration saw the world in black-and-white terms, as if this planet were merely an arena for combat between the United States and the Soviet Union. For those who shared this stark view of the world, every tremor of revolution in Chad, Grenada, or Nicaragua required a U.S. response, regardless of how small the nation, how large the loss of American lives, or how extensive the drain on the federal treasury. The US$6 trillion spent in Iraq and Afghanistan from 2003 to 2021 could have set the sagging U.S. economy aright, met the pandemic challenge more effectively, and bolstered America's homeland defenses. A thoughtful critic of American foreign policy, journalist Thomas L. Friedman understands the importance of defeating terrorist organizations, but not the expenditure of U.S. taxpayer money in a futile effort to "make Afghanistan into Norway." That goal, he has written, is simply too expensive "when balancing our needs for nation-building in America."

Beyond the financial costs of excessive intervention abroad lies the growing realization that Americans can exercise only a limited influence on the affairs of other nations. The experiences of the United States in Vietnam provide an example that should have been seared into the nation's memory. Consider the sacrifices made by the United States in Indochina during the 1960s and 1970s. More than 58,000 GIs were killed and 153,300 injured, along with the untold numbers who continue to suffer from the effects of Agent Orange and other chemical defoliants used during the war, as well as from lingering psychiatric disturbances. Yet the wide range of overt and covert force used by the United States proved unable to curb the corruption of the South Vietnamese government, unite its army into an effective fighting force, or defeat the North Vietnamese.

It would be foolhardy to seek a return to isolationism, despite the many pressing needs here at home. Two world wars have taught Americans the futility of trying to escape from the world, however tempting that may be. Like it or not, the United States is inextricably bound to the other nations of this planet. Instead, Washington must adopt a more prudent and discriminating foreign policy, "intervening" overseas initially with brigades of school and home builders; with nurses and physicians; with teachers, farmers, and economists; with the diplomats of the Foreign Service; and with the Peace Corps; and only in the most dire circumstances with the CIA or the Marine Corps.

Much of what the United States can achieve in the developing world does not demand great expense. The work of the Carter Center in Atlanta to eradicate the Guinea worm in Nigeria and Ghana offers an excellent illustration of what can be achieved without exorbitant costs. Under the Center's leadership, illness cause by the Guinea worm has been eradicated – only the second disease ever eliminated (along with smallpox). As journalist Kristof notes, "The Guinea worm campaign underscores that a determined effort, with local people playing a central role, can overcome a scourge that has plagued humanity for thousands of years."

Further, high on the U.S. foreign policy agenda should be a determination to stop global warming, the gradual increase in the earth's temperature that is caused by the entrapment of gases inside the upper atmosphere instead of their escape into space. The major culprit in creating this "greenhouse effect" is a gas, carbon dioxide (CO_2), emitted into the air by burning coal, oil, and other fossil fuels. In the past decade, this planet experienced the hottest period since modern records have been kept. One remedy is to provide better stewardship over the world's forests, which are disappearing at an alarming rate. Trees act as sponges to absorb carbon dioxide, thereby slowing global warming – an ecological process crucial to the survival of life on earth. Destruction of tropical forests around the world is estimated to account for about 20 percent of greenhouse gas emissions.

Moreover, among the lost flora in the forests may be yet undiscovered plants that contain wondrous cures for human disease. Take, for example, the rainforests in the African nation of Madagascar, the fourth largest island in the world, which has 14,000 species of plants – most existing nowhere else on earth. The Madagascar periwinkle, discovered by botanists in these rainforests, contains a substance that has been successful in treating leukemia in young children. Yet some 90 percent of the island's forests have been sacrificed to slash-and-burn agriculture, with unknown losses in potentially important plant-based medicines.

Guiding maxims for a new American foreign policy

The Trump presidency (2017–2021) saw a strong strain of isolationism returning to the United States. The president sought to withdraw America's troops from Afghanistan and Iraq, the locations of America's "forever wars," along with lowering the number of U.S. soldiers in Germany. He called into question the value of NATO, and ripped up key international agreements, such as the Paris climate accords and the pact with Iran designed to curb its development of nuclear weapons. In contrast, the new president, Joe Biden, quickly reinstated America's participation in the Paris pact, lifted Trump's travel ban for people from majority-Muslim nations, and moved to restore U.S. support for NATO and strengthen America's ties to allies throughout the world. "America is back, ready to lead the world," Biden proclaimed. Multilateralism would again replace unilateralism – Trump's "America First" approach to solving the world's problems.

Whether Republican or Democrat, it had become clear that Americans had grown wary of wars in the Middle East and wanted to concentrate more on problems at home, especially ministering to the ailing economy and eradicating COVID-19. In this sense, the internationalist Biden, too, would have to turn inward, although trying at the same time to repair the damage Trump had done to America's global network of alliances. It was a balancing act and Biden had the experience in high office (Senate, vice presidency), as well as the wisdom, to pursue an equilibrium between addressing both domestic and foreign challenges.

As the United States marches forward it could profit from closer adherence to five maxims that apply to relations between the executive and legislative branches inside the United States, as well as to America's ties to other nations overseas:

Listen

German Chancellor Helmut Schmidt once complained that Washington's idea of "consultation" was to tell him over the telephone what American was going to do. "And they called that 'consultation'!" he said. The U.S. Ambassador to the UN and the 1952 and 1956 Democratic presidential nominee, Adlai Stevenson II, suggested that the most important instrument of American foreign policy was a hearing aid: listening better to the ideas and hopes of other nations around the world. The first step in being a good world leader is to turn up the volume on that hearing aid.

Help

Secretary of State Dean Rusk recalled a trip he made to Africa in the 1960s. In a village he visited, the tribal leader took him to his hut. It was sparsely decorated, with only one adornment on the walls: a photo of President John F. Kennedy. The leader explained how important Peace Corps volunteers had been to his village, especially in the development of an irrigation system that tripled the agricultural yield for his people. The United States had gained the lifelong friendship of an Africa village. What can the United States do that will be helpful to others around the world? That is how moral standing is achieved, allies won, and America made safer by a global network of friendships.

Set a good example

Assassination teams, deadly dart guns, mining foreign harbors, the use of torture – these are not the kind of activities that Americans have traditionally held high. On the contrary, the United States is the nation that supported the Marshall Plan; sends hospital ships around the world to care for the afflicted poor, including the U.S. Navy's *Mercy* and *Comfort* that have helped tsunami, earthquake, and hurricane victims in Indonesia, Haiti, and Puerto Rico, among other locations; and champions international human rights. "If America has a service to perform in the world – and I believe it has," observed a chairman of the Senate Foreign Relations Committee, J. William Fulbright, "it is in large part the service of its own example."

Seek consensual solutions

The world is simply too vast and dangerous a place for America to go it alone; allies are essential in the struggle against global terrorism, pandemics, and environmental degradation. The United States must seek partnerships for the advance of democracy and world peace, and this in turn requires working well together – the basic lesson taught in kindergarten but too often forgotten afterward. Understanding this, President Joe Biden promised in his Inaugural Address of January 2021 to "repair our alliances." In this difficult world, the fulfillment of dreams requires collective action.

Practice the Golden Rule

Finally, as every major religion in the world extols, humans need to treat one another with respect. For personal behavior, and foreign policy, there exists no more important guideline than the Golden Rule: treating others as one would like to be treated oneself.

Notes

On making the world a better place, see Al Gore, *Earth in the Balance* (New York: Penguin-Plume, 1993); John G. Ikenberry et al., *The Crisis of American Foreign Policy* (Princeton, NJ: Princeton University Press, 2009); Joseph E. Stiglitz, *Globalization and its Discontents* (New York: Norton, 2003); Stephen M. Walt, *Taming American Power* (New York: Norton, 2005); and Fareed Zakaria, *Ten Lessons for a Post-Pandemic World* (New York: Norton, 2020). For the quotes: Kennan, *American Diplomacy, 1900–1950* (Chicago: University of Chicago Press, 1971): 79; Weinberger, interviewed by John Hughes, "Lunch with Cap," *Christian*

Science Monitor (September 12, 1986): 16; Carter, "The United States Must Guide Third World toward Self-Sufficiency," *Atlanta Journal and Constitution* (December 3, 1988): A23; Friedman, "This I Believe," *The New York Times* (December 2, 2009): A33; and Nicholas D. Kristof, "Winning the Worm War," *The New York Times* (April 20, 2010): A25. Rusk related the African village story to the author on July 4, 1985, in Athens, Georgia; and the Fulbright remark on the power of example comes from the senator's remarks in the *Congressional Record* (May 17, 1966): 10808. On the Navy's ships of mercy, see Karen J. Greenberg, TomDispath.com (December 20, 2018). "In everything, do to others what you would have them do to you ..." reads the Matthew 7:12 version of the timeless Golden Rule prescription.

Index